WHE

ENGINEERS

DARE

Janice & Tony Rayns

enjoy.

ISBN-13: 978-1-6863-4875-4

The stories in this book reflect the author's recollection of events. Some names have been changed to protect the privacy of those depicted. Dialogue has been re-created from memory.

ACKNOWLEDGEMENTS

Two and a half years after starting work on 'Where Engineers Dare' we now know that coming up with the idea for a book was the easy part. We couldn't have finished it without the help of a lot of people. Firstly, friend and author Eilidh McGinness for giving us the confidence to have a go. Thanks also to Viccie Corby and the members of the Bordeaux Writers Group for their encouragement and feedback, especially Debbie O'Neill for taking the time to be our beta reader. We are very grateful to Chuck Grieve for giving so freely of his time and expertise to help us develop our first draft into something so much better. Thanks also to Alan Hamilton for his editing skills and Les Charles for getting his sketch book and pencils out of retirement to provide the cartoons. Finally thanks to Ian Rayns for having the IT skills required to turn a sketch into a book cover. Thank you to you all. We couldn't have done it without you.

Contents

Engineer Caught Short

For over forty years I've roamed the earth as an engineer. I've been in some hot spots, some embarrassing spots, some seriously dangerous spots, and, as I start off here, some very messy spots.

It started with a bit of an inner rumble, followed by a gurgle and then everything went quiet, maybe a bit too quiet. I glanced at my watch. 7.55 am. Veer Singh, my driver, was due any minute. On the face of it, a humdrum day for a project manager. A crane inspection on a site just a couple of hours away by car. Well, it would've been run-of-the-mill, except I was in India with a belly that rhymes with Delhi.

Half an hour into the journey and the pressure was building. As we passed the half-way point, desperation started to bite but I urged Veer Singh to press on.

My growing discomfort, not to say, desperation, my inability to suppress the groans arising from my churning stomach and associated griping, became obvious to the man in the driving seat. Suddenly, he stopped the car and pointed to some bushes. Even with my limited grasp of Hindi I managed to get the message across that I needed to do something more substantial than a piss. A painfully long ten minutes later Veer Singh came back indicating he knew where I could go. In front of me, extending for almost as far as the eye could see was a six-foot-high perimeter wall. He guided me through a hole in the brickwork to a ten-foot square outbuilding and then through another gap where I guess a door had once hung. In the corner I spied a stand-up, hole in the floor, toilet. As I went to drop my trousers and let it all out, my body did what only the human body can do at such times, it went two seconds too early so that my trousers and underpants were barely around my ankles. On the plus side fifty percent of it made it into the hole. The remaining fifty percent was running down my legs and into my trousers and shoes.

In the absence of any toilet paper I got my trusty cotton handkerchief out of my trouser pocket and attempted to mop up. Minutes into the operation it became clear to me that there's a limit to how much sloppy shit a single hankie can mop up and it's considerably less than fifty percent of a full load. I saw a tap on the wall in front of me. 'Aha', I thought

and waddled across to it, trousers round my ankles, hankie in hand ready to wash out. It squeaked as I turned it on – and then the sound of silence. I now had a shitty arse, legs, trousers, handkerchief, and hands. I summoned Veer Singh and, after some further communication difficulties, sent him on the hunt for the Indian equivalent of some dock leaves. By the time he arrived back I'd made a bit of progress wiping up the mess with some lower denominations of rupee notes from my wallet.

Clean up completed to the best of my ability, I set off, walking like a cowboy who had lost his horse, to inspect the crane. A considerable amount of crap had just fallen out of my arse but it was nothing compared to the state of the crane. There was no brake on the slew around so the driver had to release the power whilst slewing and guess where to stop. Fortunately, he seemed to know what he was doing.

It was a fifteen-minute walk back to the car during which the searing June heat seemed to increase exponentially. My trousers had a crusty starched feel to them. Veer Singh refused to let me in until he had found some plastic sacks for me to sit on which added a new sweaty dimension to my discomfort. Back at the hotel I waddled up to the reception desk to fetch my key, rustling like an empty crisp packet and smelling like a sewage farm. Thankfully, Mr Chakrobarthy, the receptionist, wasn't in the mood for small talk. I sat on the toilet in the sanctuary of my hotel room for the rest of the day, wondering how my life had turned, quite literally, into such a pile of shit.

I decided 1977 had been the start of it. The Queen celebrated her Silver Jubilee, Concorde started flying between London and New York and Marc Bolan died way too young. It was also the year I launched my career into the power generation industry. I was twenty-one, and a firm in my home town of Nottingham took me on as an Assistant Project Engineer. So began my steady ascent up the engineering ladder and over the years I wore many hats, most of them white and plastic. Contracts Engineer, Project Engineer, Commissioning Engineer, Sales Manager, and Project Manager were just some of the titles I held during my career. The locals I worked with had a few others for me. Finally, I reached the dizzy heights of Managing Director of my own company. It took a lot of blood, sweat, and tears to achieve this, predominantly sweat. I've worked in some seriously hot climates (fifty degrees plus) but the humidity on a job in Qatar was the worst I have ever endured. After 30 minutes stooped over an electrical junction box in my plastic hat I stood up and a pint of sweat cascaded over me like a hot shower but without the soap. Probably just as well as soap has caused me to get into a lather more than once over the years, but I'll get to that later. It was once I was running my own company that I became virtually nomadic, a view the Passport Office shared when it agreed to issue me with a second valid passport. This allowed the visa application for my next assignment to be processed while I was already working out of the country.

However, the longest period of time I ever spent working away was back in the mid-1990s. As I remember, interest rates had hit 15% following Black Wednesday, eye-wateringly high for anyone with a mortgage, and Pop group D:Ream, featuring Brian Cox (yes, that one – the prof. who explains complex physics to us dumbos) on keyboards, were singing 'Things Can Only Get Better'. I was inclined to hope they were right. My marriage of thirteen years had just gone to the dogs. As always, neither party was blameless. Living together in the marital home was becoming increasingly fraught, so when a colleague offered to rent me his flat in nearby Chesterfield, I moved out. I figured putting some distance between us physically and emotionally would help, but it soon became apparent that Chesterfield wasn't anywhere near far enough. When a job as a Resident Project Manager in India came up within the company I worked for, it seemed like an answer to all my problems. So in the Spring of 1995, I landed in Delhi.

The India I had read about in the travel brochures was 'a colourful and exhilarating country with awe-inspiring historic monuments.' The India I landed in was dripping with humidity and stank of poverty, inequality, and cardamom. On exiting the airport, I was thrown into a heaving mass of people while my senses were assaulted by a cacophony of sights, smells, and noise. By far the loudest sound was the traffic. Bikes, rickshaws, motorbikes, Morris Oxford cars out of the 1950s, buses (packed with passengers inside and festooned with others outside), and oxen pulling carts, all jostled for position on the roads. Horns blared constantly, none of the vehicles appearing to have working indicators. I'd been told to meet my driver outside the terminal. I guessed he was the guy holding the card with 'Mr Tony' written on it, and headed over.

Driving in India is neither for the law-abiding nor the fainthearted. If the estimated toll of 550 deaths per day is correct, then India alone accounts for fifteen percent of all global road fatalities. Quite an achievement. Fortunately, I was viewed as a valuable commodity by my employer. Not wanting the inconvenience of my death or, more likely, the delay while a replacement arrived, it was company policy for a manager to be assigned a driver. That's how I came to meet Veer Singh, a tall, skinny, silver-haired guy probably in his late forties, but hard to tell. He always dressed smartly, always spoke politely, and occasionally a smile crept across his pockmarked face, but he never laughed, at least not in front of me.

Veer Singh was the proud driver, though not the owner, of a spotless Hindustan Contessa. This was a Vauxhall FE Victor in disguise as after the last ones rolled off the UK production line in the late 1970s, Hindustan Motors bought the tooling. Up to then, Hindustan had been producing a 1950s Morris

Oxford they called the Ambassador. They hailed the Contessa as a luxury car and it came in any colour you wanted so long as it was white. It did sport one new addition, air conditioning, rarely needed in an English summer, but an essential item for foreigners battling against the relentless Indian heat. Veer Singh had made a few upgrades of his own. The sweat-inducing brushed nylon seats had cotton covers, and hanging from the mirror was the obligatory Ganesh.

The first six months on the job were a bloody nightmare. It soon became obvious that things didn't happen quickly in India. We had a European client, a European contract and a European deadline which would have been fine had we not also had an Indian manufacturer and Indian site installation. I suspect that because the American parent company had an interest in an Indian manufacturing company, they were keen to keep the money within the group, which at least on paper made good business sense.

India has two unlimited resources, time and cheap manpower (or to be more precise by today's standards) labour, as the workforce included women with babies strapped to their backs who were employed to fetch and carry. Why would factories invest crores (millions) of rupees in capital equipment to move things more quickly through their works when they have an endless supply of inexpensive labour? A Project Manager has the acronym PM but it wasn't long before I changed this to PP for Pissing-Post in view of the flak I received each time I tried to explain the reason for the latest delay at the Project Progress Meetings.

During my eighteen months being urinated on, a German guy called Reiner Hoffman, the client's representative in their Delhi office, made my life even more miserable. He was vertically challenged, in his early fifties with a seriously lived-in face and waspish manner. It was fair to say that international relationships between us were even more strained than during a Brexit negotiation when each fortnight we drew pistols at the Project Progress Meeting. My problem stemmed from the fact that the two Australian guys who reported to me on the job couldn't answer him directly for commercial reasons, so all the responses had to come through me. Wanting to appease the situation, we invited him over to our hotel for a few drinks. My colleagues weren't stereotypical Australians. Bruce senior was half-German and Bruce the Greek was, well I think you can work that one out for yourself. After a typical happy hour in the bar from 6 to 8 pm, things were going well. We carried on drinking till midnight at which point the two Bruces deserted me, leaving me with our guest. Reiner then declared he wanted another drink. The only way to get one after midnight was to order room service, so it was back to mine. When this finished at 2 am, we hit the mini bar. By 4.30 am there was a solitary can of cola loitering in the fridge. Reiner took this as his cue to call his driver, and left.

I attended our next meeting in a more relaxed state, feeling that we had bonded. Unfortunately for me, Reiner was now sober. He asked whether I'd been to view the crane pre-booked for the site installation due to commence in two months' time.

My reply, 'No, not yet, there's plenty of time', was greeted with a thump on the desk.

'Mr Tony Rayns, this is India. You must go and see the crane before the next meeting.'

Keen not to strain international relationships further, I made arrangements to view the crane at 10.30 am the next day, blissfully oblivious to the shitty mess I would soon find myself in. Thank goodness for Veer Singh. His next rescue mission involved a much more serious situation.

Engineer in the Hot Seat
'...in India's sunny clime...'

The drive from my makeshift home at the Surya Hotel in Delhi to the manufacturing facilities in Faridabad took about an hour depending how many accidents there were along the way. My two Australian colleagues also lived at the Surya so it made sense to share my driver, Veer Singh, and travel together. Faridabad wasn't in what the Yanks call a 'dry' state at the time but still the laws relating to the sale and consumption of alcohol were a lot more stringent than in the UK. You had to be on licensed premises to buy *and* drink it. On our hour's journey back through the wilderness the desolate landscape was intermittently punctuated by bottle stores each selling the three essential beverages of Kingfisher beer, Coke, and Bagpiper whisky. It wasn't long before we incorporated a regular stop off at one of these stores to pick up some liquid refreshment for our trip home.

Where my Australian counterparts did match the stereotypical image was how they liked their beer - cold, bordering on crystallisation cold, whereas in those days I wasn't really a lager drinker at all, preferring something just a bit below UK room temperature. We were soon on first name terms with Sandeep who ran our bottle store of choice and each day he had two large bottles of beer just off freezing, and one 'pommie' beer in the fridge waiting for us. These he served in their obligatory brown paper bags. The two Bruces showed no hint of sensitive teeth as they polished off their lagers long before we arrived back.

One sweltering July afternoon, I had to leave site early for a meeting in Delhi and, as usual, Veer Singh picked me up. Not long into our journey disaster struck in the form of a nearside front puncture. We pulled up at the side of the dual carriageway which led into Delhi and it was like an oasis. Nothing for miles, except 300 yards away a bottle store. Veer Singh was going up in my estimation. I left him getting the jack out while I sauntered over to the shop and picked up a beer, supplied of course in its obligatory brown paper jacket. When I arrived back Veer Singh had started changing the wheel with the speed of a slow-motion mime artist. The heat in India ensures nothing happens fast so I stood leaning on the offside rear wing watching the traffic go by as this was fractionally less boring than supervising Veer Singh. We were at the side of a busy four lane road surrounded by empty land. As I supped my beer out of the bag my mind began to wander.

The rumble of a motorbike pulling up alongside me disturbed my blissful state. It was closely followed by a revolver being thrust at my chest and finally a lanyard and badge identifying the guy attached to them as a member of the Indian police. I also very clearly heard the words – in English – 'You are arrested', being repeated several times.

Ever resourceful, I shouted 'Veer Singh', my voice just tinged with an underlying hint of panic. He sprang up from behind the car like a tightly-coiled jack being released from its box. After a brief exchange he followed the policeman over to the shade and privacy of a nearby tree to carry on their conversation, not that I understood a word of what was being said. I let out a sigh of relief as the gun was returned to its holster and Veer Singh sauntered back over to me.

'Mr Tony, Sir, he says you are a very bad man. He is seeing you drinking the beer in a place most public.'

'No, I'm not.' And I hid the beer behind my back like a guilty schoolboy caught out by a teacher. He rewarded me with one of his rare smiles.

'Mr Tony, Sir, this is very serious matter, very serious indeed. I am needing to ask you if you have any money with you?'

A question to which he already knew the answer.

'How much?'

It appeared that 300 rupees, the equivalent of five quid, was the price to look the other way, an amount I was more than happy to pay. Veer Singh marched back over and exchanged some more dialogue before discreetly handing over the money. The policeman rode off on his 1950s Royal Enfield motorbike without another word, the only trace of his visit an obligatory oil patch on the road where he'd parked. Seeing my white face, he knew he could make a quick buck out of my misdemeanour, a recurring theme on my travels. He'd even left me with my bottle of beer but I drank the rest in the back of the car with it still jacked up.

* * * * *

Veer Singh wasn't always on hand to rescue me and the case of Harjit's legs was one of those times.

Living in a hotel in India may sound like a dream, no bed making, cooking, laundry or cleaning, your curtains drawn each night, and a chocolate on your pillow, but believe me, the novelty soon wears off. The hotel accommodated a lot of 'Billy no mates' (single male guests) like myself and once a month threw a Residents' Only evening function with free food and drinks. As my time in India went on, I found that as well as missing family and friends, when I was alone, most of my time was spent in male company. Still reeling from my recent marital split, I had no desire to embark on another relationship but I did miss the softer, less vulgar company of the fairer sex. Harjit was the Lobby Manageress at the Surya Hotel. She was attractive to the eye, pleasant to talk to and also attended the Residents' Only evenings. Not surprisingly I decided to seek out her company.

The place to be seen in in Delhi at the time was the Coffee Shop at the Hyatt Regency Hotel. It was a vision of opulence with its brightly coloured soft-furnishings and hand carved chairs adorned with gold. Twenty-four hours a day its huge buffet tables provided, for a price, a feast fit for a king or a hungry foreigner. However, the real *pièce de résistance* was its tantalising menu of European style pastries and cakes, the finest selection I've ever seen. At one function I bit the bullet and asked Harjit if she would like to go for tea with me. Her disappointing response was that it was not possible. We spent the following month exchanging pleasantries in the lobby. At the next residents' bash, I bit another bullet and asked her out again, being rewarded with a more promising 'Perhaps.'

A week later I bumped into her in the lobby and got a surprise invitation to go to the cinema.

'Yes of course. What would you like to go and see?'

Next door to the hotel was a cinema called 'New Friends Colony' which showed all the latest Bollywood films. I knew we would be spoilt for choice.

Her reply puzzled me. She said either we could pick something together, or maybe Mr Chakrobarthy, one of the receptionists (or Clark Kent as I called him because of his resemblance to Superman), would like to.

Still puzzled, I asked why Mr Chakrobarthy would need to choose.

'He's coming with us, of course.'

I asked if we could go on our own, but apparently it was an evening out with Clark Kent or not at all. Needless to say, even my burning desire to see a Bollywood blockbuster couldn't sell that night to me.

Next morning, I mentioned to Rajesh, the factory owner's son, what had happened. He explained the cultural issue to me.

'Sometimes, Tony, when in Rome you have to do as the Romans do. It is normal in our culture for a woman to have a chaperone when she first goes out with someone. She may be allowed out without one but this is based on how comfortable the woman is in your presence and how honest the family think you are.'

Not honest enough by the looks of it.

Ever persistent, at the next monthly function I mentioned that my invitation to go to the coffee shop was still there if she was interested but I would not be inviting Mr Chakrobarthy. To my surprise, she said she would like to go the following Tuesday and arranged to meet me in the hotel lobby at 4.15 pm shortly after her shift finished.

I looked forward to Tuesday with increasing interest and left work at 2.30 pm to allow plenty of time to get back to the hotel for a shit, shave, shower, and shampoo. At 4.10 pm I was in place in the lobby seated opposite reception waiting for Harjit. Up until this time I had only ever seen her wearing her hotel uniform of a traditional Indian sari in green, red, and gold. I was shocked when she appeared from behind the reception desk in Western dress especially as Westernisation was only just coming to India in 1995. She looked lovely but as she made her way across the lobby towards me it was her bare legs that I couldn't take my eyes off. Her skirt was cut daringly to just above the knee and protruding from it were the hairiest pair of objects I had ever seen in my life. Being a westerner, I was used to women inflicting varying degrees of torture on themselves in order to remove all bodily hair deemed to be unsightly.

We exchanged pleasantries and went to the comfort of the Hyatt Regency Coffee Shop where I spent the brief moments when I wasn't staring at her legs scanning the room in the vain hope Veer Singh was somewhere and would come to my rescue. I didn't arrange to meet her again but made a mental note to see if Clark Kent still fancied catching a Bollywood blockbuster.

* * * * *

Living on my own in a hotel room in India was miserable even on a good day. Six months in and I hit rock bottom. It was the longest time I had spent away from my three sons, Ian 11, Alex 8, and Liam 6. What I wouldn't give to cuddle up close to them or catch a glimpse of their smiling faces. Nowadays it's easy to connect instantly with loved-ones miles away. Back in the 1990s the only means of communication were letter or phone and those weren't easy. Samy, a local carrier pigeon, took the mail, and international phone calls had to be pre-booked via the operator. If the other person didn't answer it was back to square one and in the monsoon season you could forget phone calls altogether, the exchange was flooded.

My brother and sister-in-law took pity on me and booked a, for me, much-needed morale-boosting trip over. Carl, or Cocko, as he is affectionately known by the Rayns clan, is my youngest sibling. Ten years separates us, the gap filled by the arrival of my other brother Paul and sister Paula. As kids, with such a big age difference, we had little in common but once we both reached adulthood the gap shrunk and we became close both as brothers and friends. He was on hand to steady the boat when my first marriage hit the rocks and was now doing his best to ensure I didn't drown in misery after abandoning ship altogether.

They arrived at Gatwick airport to check-in for their flight with plenty of time to spare. Just as well, seeing as it was going from Heathrow. A swift taxi ride got them there in the nick of time. I soon spotted him getting off the plane. He'd broken his little toe in transit and looked like he was auditioning for a job at the ministry of funny walks. I was starting to wonder if haplessness was a genetic trait. Appearance-wise there is no doubt we're from the same stable. Both of average height, him above, me below. He's pretty much a taller, thinner, younger, hairier, version of me. Sit us opposite each other in a pair of beanie hats and we could be looking in a mirror.

I couldn't take a week off work but did manage to finish at lunchtime each day so we could spend the hot, sweaty, afternoons sightseeing. As Veer Singh, Delhi's number one driver, was already taken, I hired Balvinder, the next best thing. He was younger, probably late 20s, sported a beard and always wore a Val Doonican jumper regardless of the outside temperature. Unlike Veer Singh, he owned as well as drove a Hindustan Contessa. He ran a small hire firm and, wanting to stand out, had sprayed his car blue. It looked OK from a distance but close up there was more orange peel than at the local grove and the inside of the boot and doors were still white.

First stop was India Gate, a memorial to the 70,000 British Indian Army soldiers who died during the First World War. It could easily be mistaken for the Arc de Triomphe in Paris. A few metres behind or in front, depending which side you're standing, is a rounded dome structure called a cupola. If we had been 48 years earlier, we could have admired the statue of King George V which sat inside it but was torn down after independence.

Next up, an elephant ride for Sam, my sister-in-law. These incredible giants of the animal kingdom were magnificent. Bright painted patterns adorned their ears and faces while a bell tied to the back end warned of their arrival. I sent Balvinder in to negotiate his version of a fair price to pay. Once on board, the 'Driver' steers by tapping the back of the elephant's neck with his bare heels. This could have been a moment lifted from the travel brochure had it not all been happening at the side of the main dual carriageway. After a few paces the driver headed onto the nearside lane, giving the constant stream of rickshaws, mopeds, cars, buses, and trucks no option but to manoeuvre round his mount. Anywhere else it would have seemed out of place, but amongst the cows, ponies, oxen, dogs, and the snake charmer's errant python wandering free, the mahout and his pachyderm fitted right in.

No visit to India would be complete without a trip to feed the local rhesus monkeys. Devout Hindus believe them to be manifestations of the monkey god, Hanuman. They feed the little rascals peanuts and bananas, encouraging them to frequent public places. The monkeys reciprocate by stealing food and clothing, breaking into cars, and generally terrorising unsuspecting passers-by. It didn't take the enterprising locals long to realise there were a few rupees to be made selling peanuts to animal-loving tourists. The monkeys were a willing business partner but soon decided there was no need to wait about to be fed individual peanuts when you could easily leap on the tourists and swipe the entire bag. I deposited a big bag of nuts in my brother's hands at the earliest opportunity and it wasn't long before he was experiencing some unwanted animal magnetism.

'You've got to assert yourself', I told him, and demonstrated by staring the next monkey in the face and shouting 'boo'. The startled monkey dropped its nuts and ran off shrieking indignantly. As the next hooligan approached, my brother stood his ground and let out a loud 'boo'. The monkey treated him to a look of contempt before shouting 'boo' back and baring his teeth, at which point my brother dropped his nuts and ran off.

A trip to the Taj Mahal was a must. Words can't describe its magnificence, so I won't even try, though even in the 1990s it was very commercialised. At the entrance it's obligatory to

purchase a human tour guide. The going rate was 300 rupees, the equivalent of six quid. It sounds cheap to a westerner, but these were overinflated tourist prices. A skilled worker might only earn 125 rupees a day. The man on the lowest rung only saw part of that 300, he had to pay a cut to someone else for permission to work there, and that someone else in turn was paying another cut to the head honcho. They recite their spiel in word-perfect robotic English, but if you try and engage them in an off-script conversation, it soon becomes clear it's the only English they've learnt.

The return car trip was another experience altogether, one you'll never find in any tourist brochures. We had stopped en route for a few drinks and a bite to eat, by which time it was dusk. Balvinder was experiencing some technical difficulties with his headlights. These were operated by a switch on the dashboard which was more temperamental than a woman with PMT. He could normally coax them into working with a bit of smooth talking and flicking on and off but tonight he'd lost his touch. I was used to the roads in India. Without any street lighting, it was going to be a two-hour drive in the pitch black on a single lane track with traffic going both ways. To add to the excitement there would probably be at least one broken-down truck littering the road, normally with a fire built at the back by the safety-conscious locals to let other drivers know someone was lying in the middle of the road fixing it. With no headlights it was impossible for us to see what was in front of us or for oncoming vehicles to see us.

As our fearless driver soldiered on, we could see ahead of us, four headlights glaring and getting closer by the minute. Two belonging to a car coming towards us and another two to the one overtaking it.

'F**king hell', my brother screamed.

Balvinder swerved over as the road widened slightly, slamming the brakes on and narrowly avoiding a head-on collision. As another oncoming truck missed us by a hair's breadth, my brother regained control of his bowels and quivering legs, jumped out the car and announced he was going to walk back to the hotel. Strange how when fear kicks in, all sense of reason departs. It was pitch black, he didn't know where he was or which way to go, but it still seemed like a rational decision. This was not the cool bro I knew. I explained he ought to factor in another problem. It was the time of night when the local snakes came out of the grass to lie on the warm tarmac. He got back in the car twitching like a junkie in need of his next fix.

Ever resourceful, Balvinder pulled the connections off the switch and connected the wires together getting his sidelights and headlights on albeit without the beam. At the hotel I extracted the jabbering wreck of a brother from the car and woke my sister-in-law who had somehow managed to sleep through the whole fiasco.

Delhi had no shortage of fine eateries. At the rather pricey Bukhara Restaurant at the Maurya Sheraton Hotel we watched as its seven chefs, positioned behind a clear glass screen, conjured up a feast for us. Seated at a low table, a cotton apron covering us from knees to chin, we ate the delicious Indian delights with our fingers. I couldn't help thinking my brother's green Golden Virginia baccy tin looked a tad out of place sitting there next to the lamb bhuna.

I wanted to make our last night together special and we settled on a trip to the five star Le Meridien Hotel. It had a roof-top pool and choice of four restaurants all accessed via glass lifts which ran up the inside of a large atrium. They came complete with flashing lights and at the time were very futuristic but it wasn't the place for anyone with a fear of heights. Even twenty floors up the 'suicide' balcony only came up to your waist. We settled on the Chinese dining experience. The waiter, kitted out in a white jacket with black bow tie, showed us to our table but even at these prices you weren't immune to some bullshit. I asked why India Gate was not lit up.

'It is only lit up till 9.00 at night, sir.'

I glanced at my watch. It was 8.30 pm.

The food on the other hand was fantastic. We were just dipping into a plateful of tempura prawns when the waiter walked over and politely asked Cocko if he was Tom Hanks. We obviously knew he wasn't, but Cocko, being a bit of a wide boy, urged the waiter to lean in closer and then in a hushed voice, said, 'I am, but I'm trying to keep it quiet.'

By the time I had finished choking on my drink, the news had spread around the restaurant like a giant game of Chinese whispers. Diners and staff were looking, pointing, and waving. The brave ventured over to ask for an autograph. India's number one Tom Hanks impersonator was only too happy to oblige. He was still giving it large when we left. In the lift a couple couldn't resist asking if he would do one of his famous quotes from Forest Gump. He opened his mouth and spouted the classic 'My mom always said life is like a box of chocolates. You never know what you're gonna get.' Well they certainly hadn't got Tom Hanks. I'm not sure if the story ever made the headlines or filtered back to a confused Tom Hanks, but a lot of people went away happy that night believing they'd met him, which can't be a bad thing.

All too soon, I bade Cocko and Sam an emotional goodbye and went back to counting the days till I would be back home.

Engineer in the Making

Home for me was Nottingham, it was where I had grown up. In the Spring of 1967, along with a bunch of other ill-fated eleven-year olds, I sat the unimaginatively named eleven-plus exam. The educational authorities of the day, who had not yet incorporated the words 'comprehensive' and 'inclusive learning' into their vocabulary, were keen to stress that this was not an intelligence test. Its purpose was merely to identify the 'academically able' children and segregate them for teaching at the much sought-after grammar schools. Those deemed, at the ripe old age of eleven, to be more suited to manual and semi-skilled careers ended up in a less desirable location.

Before the reality of the eleven-plus I planned to go to grammar school and become an airline pilot. The educational authorities, though, had different ideas. If my parents were disappointed in my lack of academic ability, they hid it well. As the gates of the local grammar school were now shut firmly in my face, my misguided mother decided that attendance at the local all-boys secondary modern school, the word 'modern' being used here in its loosest sense, was the next best thing for me.

Robert Mellors School was housed in an imposing large late Victorian, or maybe early Edwardian, building. I suspect someone who passed the eleven-plus could tell you which. There was a central indoor corridor flanked by two external but covered passageways. All toilets were outside of course. The older lads congregated at 'top bogs' to smoke. 'Bottom bogs' was where years 1 and 2 went to relieve themselves but normally ended up getting their heads flushed down the pan by the occupants of top bogs.

Just as the pupils at Robert Mellors had not made the grade, the same was probably true of the all-male teaching staff who were employed primarily, I suspect, to keep order in the testosterone-fuelled corridors and classrooms. These were still the days of corporal punishment and the teachers had a whole arsenal of weapons at their disposal with which to inflict varying degrees of pain. The sound of the cane whistling through the air milliseconds before striking its target lives with me still. During the school day it added an underlying atmosphere of terror to each lesson. It's true to say I learned a lot during my years at the secondary modern but nothing that helped me pass any exam.

My form teacher was a huge ex-Sergeant Major bulk of a man who constantly patrolled the class room, his pristinely polished shoes creaking on the wooden floor. On one tour of duty he stuck his head between me and my classmate and shouted,

'Rayns! Get out.'

I dutifully made my way to the front of the class.

'Turn out your pockets', he ordered, and as I did, he appraised each item with a cruel quartermaster's eye. They were all essentials for any twelve-year-old boy. Paper clips: four. Rubber bands: two, stretched: one long, one short. Magnet: one, horseshoe. Marbles: three, two cat's eyes, one agate: chipped.

'Touch your toes.'

I knew what was coming.

From the desk drawer he pulled out his personal weapon of choice, the largest plimsoll that Woolworth's stocked. It was so big that it wouldn't have looked out of place on the foot of Coco the Clown, and from past experience I knew that as it hit you on the backside the end of it wrapped round far enough to deliver an additional blow to the side of your thigh. The only question now remaining was how many whacks. It could be anywhere between two and six, and that day I counted to six. As I returned to my desk, he called out my unfortunate classmate for a repeat of the whole scenario. Sadly, like any repeat, all suspense was gone and he knew exactly what was coming.

As we sat down together, our smarting backsides deflecting heat off each other, our teacher placed his head between us and said in a whisper,

'I could have sworn I smelt peppermint.'

I learned two very useful lessons that day. Firstly, six lashes of the slipper hurt considerably more than two, and secondly, in life you don't always get what you deserve.

I had a slight reprieve from the joys of school when I broke my leg during a football match. I heard it snap and was in agony but as the school day was nearly over, the teachers bundled me into the back of one of their cars and dropped me off at home. My parents called an ambulance which successfully sought out every pothole en route to Accident and Emergency. I was deposited in a wheelchair, my injured appendage resting on a wooden plank sticking out in front of me. An X-ray confirmed my diagnosis of a break and the doctor sent me down to the Chamber of Horrors, also known as the Plaster Room, to have a non-weight bearing full-leg plaster applied. As luck had it, we saw my Uncle Terry at the hospital and got a lift back with him. Uncle Terry's latest passion wagon was a Sunbeam Alpine, admittedly a very smart sports car but not ideal for two adults and one child with a plastered leg. I was shoehorned into the back while Uncle Terry painstakingly retraced the ambulance's pothole-ridden route back home.

The discomfort I suffered in the back of the car was nothing compared to the indignity the next day brought. Unable to manhandle me out of bed my resourceful mother called in two of the local 'dustbin men' to hoist me up and deposit me in a chair in the lounge. Worried what might happen when I needed to use the toilet, I quickly got to grips with the wooden crutches the hospital had supplied. I made an uneventful recovery soldiering dutifully to the hospital every two weeks. At the end of four weeks an X-ray showed the obligatory knitting needle stuck down the plaster but nothing else. By six weeks a twelve-inch wooden ruler was keeping it company, but my fracture was healing well although I could feel the plaster starting to weaken at the ankle. The doctor reassured me he would sort this out and gave me a handwritten paper slip to take down to the Plaster Room. On it, a single word, 'Wheel'. I sat outside waiting my turn, my imagination in overdrive. How was I going to get to school with a wheel on my foot? Would it be scooter size or bike size? Surely two or four would be easier to get around on. My turn arrived and after forty minutes a much happier lad left the Plaster Room in a long leg cast with a walking heel. It was another six weeks before I managed to retrieve my ruler.

I opted not to stop on at school after the fourth year to take my CSEs. It was the norm for A-stream students who were leaving early to be moved down to the B- stream. Things didn't get off to a good start as on the first day back I found myself sitting next to Paul Smith who had also dropped down from the A stream. Smithy was very religious and aspired to become a vicar. He kept his head down and was never in trouble with the teachers. I feared I might die of boredom before the year finished.

I cheered myself up with the thought that before the end of term I'd have it in for Danny Butcher. Throughout my school life daily skirmishes were just an inconvenience, but a constant thorn in my side was a lad who went by the name of Danny Butcher. He was one cheeky sod and early on I'd decided he needed a warning shot across his bow, so I dobbed him on his button. I didn't know he had a brother in the year above me. Bobby Butcher was built like a navvy, broad and stocky, and didn't take kindly to me landing one on his brother's nose. Bobby packed a solid punch, something I decided I didn't want to be on the receiving end of again anytime soon. So, for three years, I endured Danny's cheek. I bided my time till the end of the third year when Bobby left. Yes, Danny Butcher was definitely going to get it now.

Unbeknown to me, the lads of B stream always made the teachers' tea. So, on the first morning back, two names were chosen at random from the register. My nomination came first, followed by, yes, you've guessed it – my new classmate Danny, 'cheeky sod and thorn in my side', Butcher.

As we left the classroom five minutes before break, I gave Danny a good shove hoping for a violent reaction but all I got was, 'Hey Raynsy, leave it out. This is where we can have some fun!'

The next ten minutes spent with Danny more than made up for his three years of cheek.

Danny had always been a B-stream boy and gladly showed me the ropes. Collect the big teapot from the staffroom, take it to the caretaker's office, empty it, refill it with water and boil. When boiled add half a dozen spoons of loose tea and stir. Danny also initiated me in one further step to this daily ritual as he took the top off the teapot.

'Go on then.'

I gave him a blank look so he demonstrated by gobbing in the pot. For the briefest of moments, a slight pang of guilt hit me but then the memory of my form teacher's size thirteen slipper hitting my backside flashed through my mind and I spat out a big green one. Danny took the delicious tea up to the staff room while I took a moment to reflect that sometimes in life you get exactly what you deserve.

Yes, I certainly had a different view of a few things by the end of my time in B- stream. Take our teacher, Keg. He always taught the B stream lads so before the fourth year I'd only passed him in the corridor or seen him on playground duties. He was an unassuming, roly-poly, slightly comical looking guy, his high waisted trousers held up by braces and this in the days before Simon Cowell attempted to make it fashionable.

During a lesson one of the long-term B-streamers, Andy, was buggering about. Andy had narrowly escaped being put in Form 1R when he arrived at the school, and, yes, that R was used as an abbreviation for Retard. Keg ordered him to get out while he reached into his bottom drawer for Coco the Clown's other slipper. Andy was bigger than Keg and refused to bend over and line up his backside for the forthcoming strike. He threw a punch. Keg waved it away and then invited Andy to have another go. Andy gladly accepted but missed again at which point Keg pummelled him with a relentless barrage of blows to his body. We all looked at each other with big eyes, each silently saying 'is anyone going to help Andy' but nobody did and I never found Keg comical again.

I left school aged fifteen with no formal qualifications and even fewer aspirations, but on the plus side I was proficient in fighting, swearing, underage drinking, and enduring large amounts of physical pain.

Raleigh bikes, one of the oldest cycle manufacturers in the world, was a big employer in Nottingham at the time so I applied to be taken on as an apprentice toolmaker. I had had a previous love affair with Raleigh when, as a lad of fourteen, they produced every boy's dream machine, the Raleigh Chopper. It came in five colours, orange, green, blue, yellow and purple, green being my preference. They were so popular the shops couldn't keep up with demand, but a family friend worked as a tool setter at Raleigh and got one from the staff shop for me. It was perfect, apart from being orange. Like many a young relationship, my love affair with the chopper was short-lived and a couple of years later I traded it in for a Raleigh 'Ultramatic' moped which on a good day could hit forty miles per hour downhill.

I didn't get taken on as an apprentice toolmaker first time round but landed a job on the shop floor. The first six weeks of my working life were spent in the Raleigh Operative Training Centre learning how to build a Sturmey-Archer three speed hub assembly, which isn't nearly as exciting as it sounds. At the end of this period I was timed to see how many I could build in an hour and then passed fit for the shop floor. It didn't take long for it to dawn on me that this was going to be my life from now on, a prospect that didn't thrill me, so I asked if there was anything more challenging. There was, and I was accepted onto wheel-building, a semi-skilled occupation. It was back to the Training Centre for another four weeks learning how to put spokes into bike wheels before I again passed the timed test. I spent the next fourteen months in the wheel shop but it only took the first three for me to realise that I didn't want to do this for the rest of my life either.

My wish was very nearly granted when I had a bit of a fracas on the shop floor with one of the older guys. Being the newest member of the assembly line, not surprisingly, I was also the slowest. Normally whoever finished first passed on their leftover spokes to someone who was still working. Each spoke had a nipple on one end and a thread on the other and they were presented to you like a bunch of daffodils. The guy who finished first had taken a dislike to me and threw his unused pile of spokes on my bench making a right mess.

'You can sort them out, you bastard', I yelled.

The punch he landed on me came too fast for me to see and too hard for me to feel but I did register my head, quickly followed by my torso, hitting the workshop floor. Still dazed, I staggered to my feet. My mate's dad also worked there. He ran over and grabbing me from behind turned himself into a human straight jacket in order to restrain me. The words 'let me at him' were coming out of my mouth but my brain was thinking 'for f**k's sake don't let go, with a punch like that he'll kill me.' I suppose even life on the production line wasn't without its dangers.

Although being under eighteen had its drawbacks in that there were a whole host of things you supposedly weren't allowed to do, the most frustrating, to buy a pint in a pub, and vastly less important, vote, I did find that youth had its benefits in the world of work and I was eligible to go to college on day release. I turned up to enrol in August and in the absence of any formal qualifications or a glowing report from my Secondary Modern, I was offered a place on a Mechanical Craft Practice Part 1 course starting in the September. This proved too easy, so I was moved into year two, and then the following spring applied again for an apprenticeship position at Raleigh. My squeaky-clean record in the wheel shop secured it for me and so began my four-year apprenticeship. Raleigh then sent me to a technical college to study subjects I'd never heard of including 'Thermodynamic Processes' which touches on virtually every field of physics. Even today the slightest mention of 'Latent Heat' still fills me with trepidation. I finished the college part of the course two years early, so my tutor recommended I go on to do an Organisational Studies Course. I was then left with another year to fill so they suggested I start a two-year course at Trent Polytechnic. For younger readers, a polytechnic was basically a university but not as good. Here I was to spend two nights a week studying for the Institute of Industrial Managers Certificate which would give me letters after my name. While my previous studies had been a breeze, now I was suddenly well out of my depth. The first year included economics, production techniques and analysis, behaviour analysis and, just for fun, statistics. Anyone who has attended evening classes after a day of work will know that sometimes you're pretty knackered and even a perpetual draft blowing through the ill-fitting windows or an enthralling array of subjects like those listed above cannot deter you from closing your eyes from time to time. Our tutor was a small man, in his late 50s with thinning grey hair and a personality equally as lacklustre. Two weeks in, an unfortunate student fell asleep and even with the tutor barking a question at him, he failed to stir. A prod from the neighbouring student had the desired effect. He was instructed to pack his books away, go home, and not bother coming back. Our tutor then announced he didn't have a problem with anyone who came to learn but if we thought it was a place we could come and grab forty winks, he and we would be parting company – and he wasn't going anywhere. All eyes were wide open.

To progress to the second year, I needed to gain a minimum of 60% in all four subjects. I struggled to pass two and failed statistics and economics spectacularly. I could re-sit them in the August, but if I failed, I wouldn't be allowed on the course in September, which I needed to enrol for immediately. Against my tutor's advice I resat both and enrolled on the second year. I scraped a pass in statistics by 2% or was it 3%? I may have worked that out wrong. And failed economics. After a final resit, which I had to take at the London School of Economics in October, it was a case of third time lucky and at the end of four years I had passed the two-year course. I returned to life in the tool room at Raleigh but after three months I had what I've read was a déjà vu moment, and thought 'I can't be doing this for the rest of my life'. Fortunately I didn't have to. Shortly afterwards my career as an engineer took off. It wasn't long before I was travelling the world and putting my size 8 work boot well and truly in it.

Engineer in Error
Getting it wrong around the world

In 2008 I landed a couple of jobs in Syria. Since I was there, civil war has brought the country to destruction and even Aleppo's UNESCO world heritage site status couldn't save it from devastation. But the Syria I visited then was beautiful, the cities of Aleppo, Homs, and Damascus being packed full of historic buildings and covered souks.

The first job took me to Nazaria and surprisingly for me passed uneventfully. It also came with an added bonus. The recreational facilities on site served a purpose if, like the predominantly Portuguese workforce, you wanted a quick beer after your shift. They were housed in a building that reminded me of a run-down youth club with its unwelcoming concrete floor, Formica topped tables, battered dartboard and pool table. But if you took the trouble to venture into Damascus, a half hour's drive away, a whole different world awaited you. There you would find an oasis called the Bunker Club. Housed in the basement of the British Embassy it was reminiscent of a gentleman's club. You had to sign in, show your passport and get a member to vouch for you but formalities over you could sit back in a comfy chair amongst paintings of spitfires and enjoy a proper pint of beer or two with Winston Churchill watching over you. When the other expat lads invited me along on their regular Thursday night excursion I didn't need asking twice. On the rare occasion we fancied a glass of gnats piss there was always the bar at the American Embassy.

My second visit to Zayzoon didn't go quite so smoothly. I was commissioning some diverter dampers on a new gas-fired power plant. A diverter damper is a piece of equipment that controls and isolates the exhaust gas from a gas turbine when it exits at about 650° C. I'd been tasked with carrying out all the preliminary checks so it could be brought into service. A taxi picked me up from the airport and took me straight to site. It was midday by the time I arrived and the admin and accommodation guy told me that I was sharing a house on the site camp. He suggested that as the other worker was on the night shift and no doubt sleeping, I should go and start my shift and then make my way to the house around 6 pm. Great plan considering I'd just been travelling for 14 hours solid.

When I arrived at my digs I was home alone. It comprised two bedrooms, two bathrooms and a communal kitchen and lounge housed in a semi-detached single floor, brick-built and rendered prefab, complete with a small front garden. Bedroom and bathroom No 1 had my name on them and I wasted no time unpacking and taking a much-needed shower. Ceramic tiles covered all the floors and with no shoes and socks on I felt an unpleasant coldness underfoot. If only I'd packed my slippers. As luck would have it, when I made my way into the communal lounge to watch a bit of telly, I noticed a rug coiled up on the settee. Perfect. I had to be on duty at 7 am the next morning and I turned in early, taking the rug with me so my feet would be greeted with something warm when I got out of bed.

I left without seeing my roommate, a Groundhog Day passed and I returned to an empty house to enjoy a few hours relaxation before bed. It didn't take me long to notice that the rug had disappeared from my bedroom and I found it once again rolled up on the settee. I assumed the room boys, who cleaned each day, had moved it, so I put it back by my bed ready for morning.

My patience was starting to wear a bit thin when I arrived back after the next Groundhog Day to find the rug once again not where I had left it. The following night, the rug was nowhere to be seen but my housemate was waiting for me.

'Hello', I said, 'I'm Tony. I'm surprised you're still here. You're late for your shift.'

'I know', he replied, without smiling. 'I have been waiting for you.'

'Is there a problem?'

"Yes, I want to know why you keep moving my prayer mat?'

* * * * *

I landed in Jordan in 2007 with my brain lagging seriously behind my mouth. My instructions were to make my way to the hotel lobby bright-eyed and bushy-tailed on the first morning to meet the client's two representatives. One turned out to be a French guy, the spit of Gene Hackman, the other a six-foot-six Dutch man-mountain. We passed a pleasant first day on site, returning to the hotel around 7 pm when Gene asks if I'm coming for a beer. A lot of Middle Eastern countries are dry but you can get a drink in the hotels so long as you are prepared to pay the rip-off prices demanded. I guess we were. The Dutch guy asks what I want. I order a beer like them before taking a seat opposite the bar. A few minutes later, the waiter arrives with a tray of three beers, two in pint jugs and the third in a ridiculously ornate glass receptacle which could have doubled as a flower vase. Being the new kid on the block, I waste no time telling the waiter,

'If that pussy glass is for me, you can take it back and bring me one of these', pointing to the two jugs. At which point, the big Dutch guy leans over, takes the ornate vase from the tray, and proceeds to drink from it. Oops.

* * * * *

While working in India, a colleague was staying at the Hyatt Hotel in Delhi, and once a month we met there on a Sunday afternoon to use the facilities (bar, pool, gym) before going to the Hyatt Coffee Shop for a bite to eat. Very rock and roll, I know. Lads being lads, we got to know the local ladies of the night who frequented the hotel lobby, although none of us used their services, honest. They'd come over if business was slow, knowing we'd stand them a few drinks. All good fun when you're out with the lads at the weekend. Not so funny though, when you're greeting the heads of the two international firms you are subcontracting for, and one of them makes a beeline for you. Awkward, but nowhere near as awkward as my visit to the sauna.

Personal hygiene is important, especially in a hot climate where Betty Swallocks (think about it) is a constant companion. Working in Delhi, Monday to Saturday, consisted of long hours, sometimes just making it back to my hotel for happy hour followed by a shower and bed. Sundays allowed the luxury of a bit of a lie-in and a leisurely breakfast and then sending in the weekly reports to the UK office. On Sunday afternoon, if it wasn't our once a month trip to the Hyatt there was a wide choice of nothing available to bore you senseless. Nowadays you could easily occupy a few hours with only your mobile for company. Call the family, google the latest gadgets and look at what people you hardly know are doing on Facebook. Back in the 1990s, phones were wired into the wall and were for making phone calls. Even the MP3 player was still a distant dream – in-room entertainment consisted solely of Indian TV. My hotel did have a pool and gym, but these were not up to much. There was a steam-room in the pool complex and although I had spent most of the week sweating in temperatures of forty degrees plus, in a moment of madness I decided to give it a try.

Being a Sunday afternoon, hotel staff were as prolific as sailors on the Mary Celeste but I eventually found it hidden in the bowels of the basement. A hand-written sign indicated a dress code of swimming trunks or a short towel. As soon as I entered, a thick fog of steam engulfed me through which I could see bugger-all. In my rush to close the glass door as quickly as possible, I became disorientated but could just make out what looked like the bottom of a marble bench about four foot in front of me. I took two short paces, turned around and sat down. The resounding shout of 'ow' which

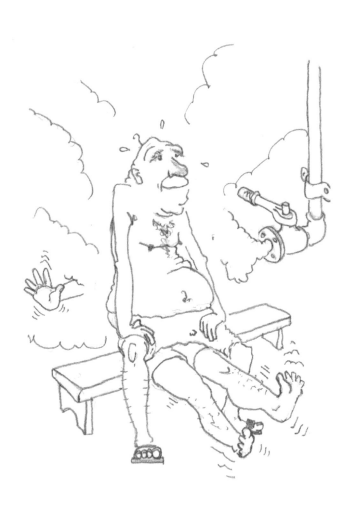

occurred simultaneously led me to believe I had sat on someone and sure enough two legs were sticking out from under my arse. My impromptu cushion moved from his prone position on the bench. Slowly, over the next five minutes as my vision became a bit clearer, I could see a guy sitting to my left and the outlines of several others. There was a valve for the steam on the wall and the bloke sitting near it said something in Hindi to my neighbour, and, agreement reached, he operated a hand lever at knee height which let out raw steam so hot it would take your skin off if you were in its path but not a concern for Indian health and safety regulations at the time. After a ten-second burst, the room was full of steam and visibility once again restored to bugger-all.

Over the next ten minutes, four people left, including the steam valve operator and as visibility was restored, I realised there was only me and the guy whose legs I had sat on left. Feeling a little awkward, I blurted out an apology for sitting on him. He took this as his cue to make conversation with me. We went through the normal enthralling routine of where I was from, what I was doing in India, how long I was there, where I was living. He then asked if I had got a woman in India. Not sure where this conversation was going, I explained at length that I was in the process of getting divorced and another woman was the last thing I needed. The awkwardness of the conversation then went up a notch as he asked me how I relieved myself sexually. Worried he was looking to fit me up with one of the local prostitutes, or worse still, offer his own services, I felt obliged to answer.

'Like every bloke does, I have a wank now and again.'

He sat up at this point and said, 'A vank. What does that mean?'

As always, my undiscovered talent as a street mime artist saved the day, and I performed the universal action. Not sure what topic of conversation to follow on with, I made my excuses and left, feeling dirtier than when I had gone in.

* * * * *

It's good to know that now and again someone else can put their foot it in. In 2007, while Harry Potter was heading off to start his fifth year at Hogwarts, I was en route to Jamnagar, in the state of Gujarat, India, to work at the biggest oil refinery I had ever seen. To give you an idea of its vastness, when my driver (yes, it's India so I've got a driver again) entered the site there was an obligatory thirty mile per hour speed limit and it took twenty-five minutes to get to my work area. I completed three, six-week stretches, each time commissioning two huge gas turbine units. The oil refinery needed all six of these units to power it.

Needless to say, I got to know a fair few of the guys on site. Rajiv was twenty-one, and looked out of place with his tall, skinny boyish frame and bumfluff beard. He was still at university and completing a period of work experience. Like many of his counterparts, his appetite for knowledge was insatiable, and he was keen to learn all he could about western life and beliefs. During one of our impromptu chats, he mentioned that as part of his course he had to research a powerful leader.

'Oh, who are you going to do?' I asked, trying to feign interest.

His response certainly got my attention.

'I've been doing some research, and that Hitler fella, he seemed like a very good man.'

Not sharing his view, I glanced over my shoulder to see who was listening and then said, 'You need to be careful who you say that in front of?'

Ever-thirsty for knowledge, his not unexpected reply was, 'Why?'

By this point I was a little curious to know what had led him to form this view of Hitler, so I asked, 'Why do you think he is a good man?'

'Well, I've read how he was a charismatic leader with a huge following in Germany and ...'

'Hang on a minute', I interrupted, already having heard more than I could stomach. 'I don't know what books you've been reading, but you need to go away and look up the Holocaust.'

He had not heard the word before, so I wrote it down and suggested he might refrain from telling anyone else what a good man Hitler was until he had looked it up.

Several weeks passed before I saw him again, but the first words he uttered were as welcome as a cup of hot cocoa on a winter's night.

'Hey, Mr Tony, that Mr Hitler, he a very bad man.'

Engineer Off-duty = Engineer Bored

The life of an engineer who works mostly abroad is one of intense but quite short periods of stress and activity bookended by much longer periods of boredom.

Inevitably, off-duty time invites the question. 'What shall I do with myself?'

Medical professionals constantly go on about the dangers of too much alcohol, yet, even in places where it's not officially available, like in most of the Middle East, or it's eye-wateringly expensive, like in Scandinavia, the bored will seek it out. As, of course, they will embrace gambling as a way to pass the time.

At the end of a particularly gruelling four-week stint of sobriety while commissioning some dampers for Rolls-Royce in the far from desirable location of offshore Angola, I made my way directly to the main terminal at Luanda Airport. The formalities of check-in dispensed with, I wasted no time heading to the bar and ordering a beer. It was a typical no-frills airport bar with about ten wooden tables dotted around, comfy but basic. As usual, I was 'Billy no mates' as I sat down at an empty table opposite the big windows overlooking the runway and savoured the first pint. Half an hour later, I strolled back to the bar and ordered a refill before dawdling back to my solitary pew.

The second pint was slipping down nicely when five guys, South African I guessed by their accents, asked if they could join me. I'd like to think it was because I looked like a happening sort of guy, but in truth the only free seats left in the bar were the ones at my table. I didn't catch all their names but their leader was a stocky guy named Kurt. They were a friendly bunch who had been working on another platform and were heading home on leave to Johannesburg on the same flight as me. Five minutes later they'd downed their first pints with the enthusiasm of a group of students on fresher's week, and when the second arrived there's also one for me. At this point I was only half way down my second pint and by the time I made a start on the third, a fourth had been plonked down in front of me by another of my newfound buddies. I figured the only way out of this was to go and buy the next round of drinks and not get myself one. A nifty move but one that didn't go unnoticed. It was with a sense of relief that, when I'd almost downed my fifth pint, I heard the flight being called. I went to make my escape but my newfound buddies stopped me.

'Don't worry they'll call us, they won't leave without us.'

Ten minutes and another round later, sure enough there was a call for us by name to go to the gate. My bladder was about to explode but no-one'd thought to allow time in the schedule for a trip to the bathroom.

On board, I contorted myself into a series of strange positions such as would make a yoga expert proud, to try and relieve the ever-increasing pressure on my bladder. I was seated in row 20, Kurt and the gang directly behind me. As soon as the plane was in the air, they were up and heading to the galley, dragging me along with them. Being regular travellers on the flight, they were on first name terms with the cabin crew who were happily serving them lager with whisky chasers before the in-flight service commenced. My protests of not wanting a short gained me the concession of being allowed a brandy instead of whisky, which I detest (sorry Scotland). It was the first time I'd spent the whole of the flight in the galley but on the plus side, at least the toilet was handy. By the time we stepped – or rather staggered – off the flight five hours later, we were all pissed. My buddies were almost home but I still had to get my connecting flight to Heathrow. I'm not sure how, but I made it through to the departure area, by some miracle continuing to be in control of my legs albeit on automatic pilot. My vision was another matter. I was now seeing double and couldn't read the information screens to find out which terminal and gate I needed, so I had to ask a passer-by who thankfully also spoke fluent Swahili. The next four hours were spent sitting on a bunch of keys, the one to my front door shoved very close to where the sun don't shine in an attempt to stop me falling into an alcohol-induced coma and missing my connecting flight to Heathrow.

* * * * *

Finding something to fill the hours over the enforced Saturday afternoon and Sunday off in India was a challenge to say the least. Sometimes on a Saturday afternoon the guys from the site would come up to Delhi. We must have looked a motley crew. There was Yorkshire Gary, Lofty Lou, who was actually even more vertically challenged than me, Big Buck, Geoff our elder brother, and Boozer Don who, despite being 60, could drink all night and still get up fresh as a daisy in the morning. Our usual watering hole was the Rodeo Bar in Connaught Place smack bang in the middle of Delhi. Connaught Place was a huge commercial and business area centred on a ring of buildings with massive stone pillars, typically colonial in style. If you were into designer shopping, you'd be in heaven. In the middle was the Central Park, an enormous formally laid out garden kept alive in the baking summer heat by a tireless array of water sprinklers. The neatly manicured grass never saw a lawnmower, a team of locals were employed to cut it using hand shears.

Connaught Place attracted the tourists, and hand-in-hand with this came the enterprising locals trying to earn a few rupees, including a man who bizarrely offered to clean my ears out for me. I walked on, pretending not to hear him. The shoeshine guys were a well-polished act to say the least. A hundred yards in front was the man employed to splat your shoes with mud before you reached them.

Underneath Central Park, accessed by a tiled stone staircase, thrived the Palika bazaar, Connaught Place's aptly named 'ugly underbelly'. A huge market – and I mean huge. There were thousands of people and you could purchase just about anything, though it was a case of buyer beware with fake and genuine items intermingling. I gave it a wide berth, mainly because its plumbing left a lot to be desired and a foul stench, the sort that lingers in your nostrils for days, permeated the air.

On the other hand, the Rodeo Bar was an unexpected oasis as Delhi didn't really have a bar culture at the time. It milked the rodeo theme to the max with saloon-style doors to the toilets and kitchen and large wooden-framed mirrors. I couldn't help thinking the massive wall-mounted TVs blaring out music and sport slightly spoilt the ambience but the tasty menu of Mexican-style food, delivered by

Indian waiters in cowboy costumes, certainly made up for it.

* * * * *

A brief liaison with gambling proved to be a painful experience for me. I should have learnt my lesson back in my youth when working as an apprentice at Raleigh bicycles in Nottingham. I had taken to playing three-card brag at the company's social club with the big boys who worked on the shop floor and whose wage packets were a lot fatter than mine. Like all gamblers who come to grief, I was so sure I had a winning hand I put my weeks wages in (a whopping £12), borrowed another £10 from the pot, followed by £20 from a so-called mate in order to find out that the guy I was convinced was bluffing, wasn't. Thankfully, I stopped short of chucking in my car keys, but only just. His prial of tens from blind beat my ace, two, three on the bounce.

It was a long time before I fell victim again, but I did. When I first arrived in India in the mid-1990s, before I was introduced to the delights of the Rodeo Bar by the site lads, trying to find something to do on a Saturday night was a challenge. The two Aussie Bruce's I worked with were married and had brought their wives over, so needless to say they didn't want me tagging along making a cosy fivesome. Thinking about it, this may have had something to do with me telling Bruce the Greek that the only thing worse than a loud-mouthed Australian was a loud-mouthed American shortly before he introduced me to Tammy, his American wife. The only other guy who was on his own was Bob Plummer, the client's representative, so we palled up. He was a good-looking moustachioed guy who fancied himself as a bit of a ladies' man.

One Saturday afternoon, we got talking to some Australian pilots in our hotel bar and learnt there was a casino and disco at another Delhi hotel, the very upmarket Maurya Sheraton, where the British Airways crews stayed overnight. The only problem was you had to be a member, but the Australians reassured us we should be able to blag our way in – they had, several times.

We headed over around 9.30 pm. Sure enough, the doorman asked to see our membership cards. I muttered something about having left mine in my room and then showed him my British Airways Loyalty Card, at which point he asked if I was British Airways staff.

'Yes', I piped up, 'And I'd like to bring a guest in.'

Mission accomplished.

Gambling in its raw state was prohibited in India but in my experience where there is a buck to be made there is a loophole to be found. In this case, if no actual money changed hands at the tables it was not illegal. As soon as we entered the casino the staff, smartly dressed in black waistcoats and ties, wasted no time ushering us towards the cashier's desk where we handed over our credit cards to purchase tokens to use at the tables.

I headed over to the blackjack table, while Bob tried his hand at roulette; our pockets stuffed full of chips marked with different denominations of rupee. Lady Luck was giving me a wide berth and twenty minutes later I had run out, so I made a return trip to the cashier's desk. This stack of chips disappeared even faster than the first lot. Bob wasn't having any better luck so we decide to kill a bit of time at the bar before the disco got going.

While struggling to enjoy my horrendously overpriced drink I got talking to Didier, the French guy next to me. He asked what I did. Not wanting to blow my cover story I told him I was a BA pilot. The one thing you don't want to happen when you are impersonating a pilot is to introduce yourself as a pilot to someone who actually is. Didier worked for Air France and was keen to discuss with me the all new airbus model. In particular he wanted to hear my thoughts on its angle of stall. Needless to say I finished my drink and made a sharp exit. At midnight Bob and I headed for the disco which was housed in the hotel's basement. I didn't go a bomb on their interior designer. All the walls were covered in garish gold, red and black floor to ceiling silk curtains. A polished brass bar ran down one side of the room while the opposite wall was filled with black leather seating. Both guided you down to the half-moon dance floor at the end of which sat the DJ booth. My attention was grabbed by the massive speakers dotted around the room the sort of things bands in the early 1960s used. It was nothing like the heaving sea of bodies you would find in a UK nightclub and too sparsely populated to allow any mingling in. I didn't feel India or Bob were ready for my dance moves just yet. I rolled into my hotel room in the early hours, turfed out the contents of my pockets onto the desk and fell into a deep sleep.

The next morning started late, and after showering I inspected the previous night's debris from my pockets. It was then that I came across the casino receipts totalling 300 quid which had been taken off my credit card. At fifty rupees to the pound the casino had proved to be an expensive mistress and not one I would be visiting again any time soon.

Engineer in a Lather

Soap, not one of life's luxury items, but an essential one in my line of work. Hard to believe that even this innocuous substance has landed me in trouble more than once. Back in the early 1980s I was working as a Project Engineer at Becorit and was called out to a breakdown after warranty at the Blue Circle cement works in Cookstown, Northern Ireland. The guy in charge, Dominic Green, was a nice old- school type who bore an uncanny resemblance to the actor Gordon Jackson, more Hudson in 'Upstairs Downstairs' than Cowley in 'The Professionals'. I took a frantic call from him one morning saying, 'they were in the shit'. One of the guillotine dampers which were used to feed cement into or out of the kilns was stuck half-way down and it was impossible to open or close it, so they had had to shut the whole plant down. Needless to say, they required someone sending over immediately if not sooner. I called

Richard, the Managing Director and owner of the company who did the subcontract manufacturing of the dampers for us. He was a hands-on guy who had come up through the tools. On hearing of the problem and not having anyone else free to send with me, promptly announced he would go.

Two hours later, and we were on the road at the start of a laborious eight-hour drive up to Stranraer to catch the night ferry to Larne. On the plus side, I was behind the wheel of my boss's new company car, a Mark 4 Cortina 1.6 GL, not yet being thought worthy of one of my own. We caught the ferry in the nick of time and after grabbing a few hours kip on board, disembarked still bleary-eyed, and headed over to site. The situation hadn't improved any, and short of a quick fix, the guys at the cement works wanted us to get the damper into either the open or closed position so they could restart production.

Prising off the top covers, Richard shone his torch and made the first appraisal.

'F**k me, Tony, you don't want to see what's gone off inside there.'

It was bad. The single screw jack had bent into an arc. We needed to remove it, take it to a workshop, straighten it to within normal limits, reinstall it, couple it up to the motor and the torque limiter, recommission it, and put the covers back on. It was 8.30 in the evening by the time we had finished, and wearily set off on the half-hour drive to the hotel the client had booked us into. We looked like extras from Casper the Ghost – white cement dust covering us from head to toe.

Desperate to get cleaned up and have something to eat, we rushed to get our overnight bags out of the boot but the key wouldn't open it. Richard declared it was too late to call anyone out and wasted no time locating a large screwdriver from the tool bag we had stashed in the rear foot well. With the aid of a brick from the crumbling outside wall of the hotel, he pushed the screwdriver inside the lock and opened the boot with the speed of a smash-and-grab robber. We got our bags and piled some more bricks on the boot lid to keep it shut.

I wasn't sure how I was going to explain this to the boss when I got back. It looked unlikely I would ever be getting a company car of my own.

Dominic, the Commissioning Manager from the cement works, was waiting for us when we arrived. We urgently needed a wash before dinner but being a small hotel, last orders in the restaurant were at nine-thirty, so we asked for steak and chips and a couple of beers ready for when we came back down. There was no shower in the room, just a bath, which I started running while unpacking my clean clothes. A knock on the door interrupted me. It was Richard. There was no complimentary soap in the room and he hadn't packed any. Luckily, I had, and despite the lack of toiletries the hotel had stretched to a bowl of complimentary fruit with a knife. I told him to get his bath running and then come back by which time I should have managed to cut my soap in half. This task was completed with relative ease, so I stripped-off and just as I was going to leave the bar of soap by the door for when he came back, there was another knock at the door.

'Come in', I shouted.

Dominic, being a thoughtful soul, had asked the hotel to send up two beers and before me stood a young, red-faced, waitress. During dinner I avoided eye contact with her, grateful that meat and two veg were not on the menu.

* * * * *

Just as too little soap can cause a problem, so can too much. Working offshore is not easy even if the accommodation does come with a 360 degree panoramic sea view. It involves being separated from family and friends for weeks at a time and, more seriously, all alcohol is banned. Recognising this, the UK, Norwegian, and Danish sectors provide as many home comforts as possible with a wide choice of hotel quality food and recreational facilities. The first time I did a four-week commissioning job offshore on a Brazilian FPSO (floating production storage and off-loading vessel), it quickly became apparent that living standards here were different and this was going to be more lorry-park than four-star luxury, even if there was a netted five-a-side football pitch on-board. Only in Brazil!

I landed on the FPSO and reported to heli admin. As a new boy on board or 'green hat', I had to complete a short induction which involved watching an enthralling DVD for an hour and then a quick tour round to see where things were including my cabin. The induction box ticked, I was escorted back up to admin to collect my bags. I was the only 'green hat' to have landed on that flight and I was somewhat bemused when the guy conducting the induction presented me with two bars of soap. Wondering if my personal hygiene was in question, I asked why.

'One is for your person and the other one for your clothes', came the matter-of-fact response.

'What do you mean, my clothes, surely you have a laundry?'

'Yes of course we do, but it is only for the washing of overalls. You have to wash your own clothes in your cabin.'

I'd only had a brief peek at my cabin but could already see a problem with this arrangement. There were four to a cabin, and as well as the bunks there was also a single shower room with a small S-shaped electric radiator with four bars each about eighteen inches long. Bunk A had the top horizontal bar, bunk B the second, bunk C the third, and bunk D the bottom. No guessing which bunk the new boy had been given. On the top three there was already a colourful array of underpants and socks. The next morning, I went out on shift and when I got back to the cabin, I noticed one of the other guys going into

TOOTH
BRUSH

the shower with his underclothes on. He proceeded to shower in them, take them off, dry off, take the dry ones off the radiator and then place the newly-washed items on the rail. All well and good for bunk A at the top, not so good for bunk C, and particularly bad for bunk D on the bottom. My almost dry pants and socks were now being dripped on by the newly washed items above. Thankfully, his freshly-washed T-shirt and trousers were draped over the chair and back of his bed. I got the feeling this was going to be a very damp week from the waist down, possibly accompanied by some type of fungal infection.

I was filled with an uncontrollable sense of excitement when I came to the end of my stint on the first FPSO and was told to be ready to disembark on the afternoon chopper which would transfer me to the other FPSO. There was a 1 in 4 chance I wouldn't get bunk D again.

It was late afternoon before the chopper took off but 15 minutes into the flight, I noticed we were turning and heading towards the mainland. We landed on shore and I was informed that there was no soggy accommodation available for me on the other FPSO so some bright spark had made the decision to abandon me and my baggage on dry land, leave me to find my own bed for the night and then rebook me on another chopper out the next day. Just when I thought things couldn't get any worse, there was a power cut and the whole of Macaé was plunged into darkness – and I mean pitch black. I retrieved a torch from my tool bag and extracted the whereabouts of the nearest hotel from a passing stranger. It was no surprise to find they were full, but my fortune changed for the better when I found a guy in the bar who was waiting for a friend to arrive. He suggested I join him for a drink and then once his mate arrived, they would take me to another hotel. True to their word, they sorted my accommodation problem and I enjoyed a comfortable night's sleep free from the sound of strangers snoring or farting and the aroma of damp laundry. Next morning, they picked me up on their way to the heliport where I checked in at 8 am and waited for my flight number to be called. Here I hit another problem. All the numbers were being called out in Portuguese and my grasp of the language only stretched to 'Please', 'Thank you' and 'I'd like a beer.' The best solution was to mime 'I don't speak Portuguese, please tell me when my number is called' to the woman on reception and sit facing her so she didn't forget about me. Each time a number was called I looked at her like an expectant puppy waiting to go for a walk. At 4 pm she called me over and after an emotional goodbye, I boarded the helicopter. It wasn't long before I was settling into bunk D on the other FPSO.

Although deficient in the personal laundry department, overall the accommodation on the Brazilian vessel ranked average. The award for the worst accommodation going is an easy choice. In 2009, I was sent on a job offshore Angola. I arrived at the heliport to find a local guy also waiting. He informed me his superiors had told him to turn up for a meeting, but judging by his attire of a smart suit and leather briefcase they had neglected to mention it involved a trip offshore.

The FPSO didn't have any space left on it, so I was told I would be sleeping on the nearby accommodation vessel. This turned out to be a converted 4000-ton supply ship which housed around 200 men, a mix of Angolan locals and Koreans. The cabins were made out of old shipping containers placed end-to-end and stacked two high, each containing four beds and a sink. The four-foot space between containers housed the toilet and shower. It was a shithole, and I tried to spend as little time as possible on it, eating in the mess on the FPSO and then transferring to the accommodation vessel at 7 pm. There was very little to do once you were on there but the local workers made their own entertainment and the biggest pastime was fishing. Many came prepared with six-foot long, thick, telescopic fishing rods. First of all, they shone a torch into the water to attract squid which they used as bait for the real prize, tuna. Anything caught was taken to the galley, cooked and shared out amongst the fishing party. Only the fins, gills and guts went to waste.

I spent many hours watching them, as it was no mean feat reeling in a tuna. One lad was wrestling with his rod for a good ten minutes trying to land his catch only for it to disappear back into the water. Undaunted he tried again with some success in that he reeled in the head with a clearly visible bite mark where a shark had helped himself to the catch. As I leant against the hand rail, checking it was secure first, I was reminded of a much earlier attempt to catch my own dinner.

It was shortly after I had left school and was working on the increasingly monotonous shop floor at Raleigh bikes. Most of my friends had elected to stay on at school and take their exams if only to postpone the impending tedium that the world of work offered, but five of us decided to go on a camping trip to Whatstandwell in neighbouring Derbyshire. My mate Lank (unimaginatively nicknamed because of his stature), persuaded his dad to make a recce of the campsites to find the ones willing to take five fifteen-and sixteen-year old lads. Not surprisingly, we were offered a choice of one, a farmer's field with no facilities except running water in the form of the river Derwent. Unbeknown to us until our first drunken night, the farmer was in the habit of sending the local gamekeeper round to quickly curtail any rowdy behaviour. He would appear in the dark of night shining his torch first on your face and then on his gun. As I look back to that damp May morning when Lank's dad dropped us off, I can't help thinking he took a bit too much pleasure announcing he'd be back in a week.

Prior to departure, drawing on the wealth of knowledge we had gleaned from our enforced time in the Cubs and the Boys Brigade, we had put together our essential camping kit. This comprised of two borrowed two-man tents, sleeping bags, a frying pan, gas bottle, fishing rods and some beer. Had we been in the Girl Guides we may have also packed food, toilet rolls, matches, cooking utensils and a torch. Luckily it was only a six-mile round hike to the village shop which, being a village shop in the 1970s, was closed between noon and two, a fact we discovered at half-past twelve on our first trek up there. On the other hand, the village pub was open but our success rate at getting served in a pub up had, until this point, not been that great. I don't know if it was the fact that the Derbyshire air had aged us in the short time we were there or the lack of an active police force over the border, but it seemed we looked much more like eighteen year-olds and got served without any hassle. Things were looking up, although our shock at getting served in the pub was nothing compared to seeing, for the first time, a bus being driven by a woman, something pretty unusual in the early 1970s.

We soon started to make the best of things, despite several failed attempts to catch a meal in the river. Instead we survived on a balanced diet of bacon sandwiches, chips from the local chippy and our essential supply of 'tinny beers' supplemented by the odd pint in the pub. We used the river to wash, piss, and shit in, the latter doing away with the need to waste our limited budget on toilet rolls.

Our ingenuity was tested to the max when a funfair appeared 500 metres down river, but unfortunately on the opposite bank. We risked life and limb to shimmy across a gas pipe two foot in diameter shrouded in spikes and barbed wire all for a ride on the waltzers and a hot dog. The return trip in total darkness was even more hazardous.

Five days in, disaster struck. The heavens opened and there was a torrential downpour. It's a good idea to check how watertight your tent is, preferably before you're sleeping in it. One of ours passed, the other failed spectacularly. The next two days were spent trying to dry out our sleeping bags and the tent on a makeshift washing line strung between a couple of trees. It's true to say that the trip brought us closer together, especially when we all crammed into our remaining dry two-man tent to sleep each night. It was certainly good training for life sharing a cabin on board an offshore platform.

Engineer in Danger

Danger comes in many guises. You can put yourself in it, dice with it or try to keep out of it, but sometimes you just can't escape it. I got my first taste of danger in India in the mid-1990s.

I was ten months into my stay and enjoying a customary pre-dinner beer at the Surya Hotel. Things ran like clockwork under the watchful eye of Lal, the bar manager. He silently supervised his team of waiters like the conductor of an orchestra. With a nod of his head or a flick of his wrist he signalled for a table to be wiped, a drink to be fetched, a refill for table five. Suddenly there was an almighty bang, loud enough to wake a sleeping politician during a commons debate. The building shook and a shower of yellow brick dust filtered down, covering me, and worst still, my beer. Another regular, American Mike, was in the corner opposite me. He started shouting that a lift had come down. My eyes focused on the inner restaurant opposite, its external windows

72

blown in, the diners showered in fragments of glass. I wasn't putting my money on the lift theory and doubted anyone would be leaving a tip in the restaurant tonight. Like a lost sheep, I joined the rapidly-forming herd of staff and guests heading for the lobby. All that was left of the cinema next door was a pile of rubble and dust – and a Sunil Shetty poster. A car bomb, planted I believe by Tamil separatists, had gone off, indiscriminately killing and maiming anyone unfortunate enough to be in the vicinity. I breathed a sigh of relief I hadn't picked tonight to watch a Bollywood blockbuster.

In the back of my mind I probably knew it was only a matter of time before the unrest got too close for comfort and I was in the wrong place at the wrong time. During my early days as a Project Manager, my boss John, an affable guy in his mid-fifties tasked me with finding an electrical store and setting up the office with all the essentials – fridge, toaster, and kettle. The closest place to go was the South Extension, the Indian equivalent of the local high street. I was already a frequent visitor to the deli housed there which as well as being a purveyor of fine Indian foodstuffs, also sold, for an extortionate price, a good selection of expat goodies. Thursday was my weekly trip to the bank in downtown Delhi and always included a detour to the deli to bring back supplies of corned beef, potatoes, and baked beans for the lads on site. Under their close supervision, the Indian camp chef would cook a simple English meal.

It's odd how after a while you miss the basic tastes of home.

An electrical shop close to the deli was able to furnish me with all the items needed to set up the office kitchen. Three weeks later, the kettle packed up so I took it along with me on my next trip to the South Extension to get a replacement. After going to the bank, I walked up the road looking for the electrical shop. I then walked back down the road before going back up the road and then, thinking I was going nuts and wondering if I was in the wrong place entirely, popped into the deli and asked there. I showed him the receipt. He nodded.

'Gone.'

'I know it's gone. Gone where?'

'No, just gone', he said, pointing at a gap and a pile of rubble between two shops.

It had been bombed. I wasn't up on consumer rights in India but I had a feeling my receipt wasn't going to be worth much and headed off to find another electrical store.

I decided the bomb outside the hotel was too close for comfort. An armed guard had been placed outside my room, which increased rather than decreased my fears. Not wanting to risk my next flight home being in a casket in the cargo hold, I wasted no time arranging my transfer to the site camp. The extra hour's travelling each day would be a small price to pay for my safety.

* * * * *

On a scale of one to ten, although frightening at the time, the events in India scored pretty low. I'd give them a three on the 'arsehole twitching like a rabbit's nose' scale. As I continued on my travels, I often found myself in places where the risk of kidnapping or murder because of the colour of your skin and your line of work were an ever-present worry.

In 2007, I arrived in deepest, darkest Pakistan to commission a diverter damper on the back end of a large Siemens gas turbine. Normally a hydraulics and programmable logic controller expert from the hydraulic package vendor accompanied me but they didn't have anyone available (or more likely no one wanted to go), so being a multitalented individual, I took on the job. The area of Sindh province was notorious at the time for targeted attacks on religious minorities including Christians. You stood a chance of being kidnapped too. The militants knew that the rich oil and power generation companies would quietly pay £10,000 for the safe return of a white European worker. Punishment was severe if caught but the chances of that happening were almost non-existent.

I flew into Islamabad and then onto Karachi, South Pakistan, from where I took an internal flight to the back of beyond. I could see the flat shanty town from the aircraft, row after row of tin huts so close to the runway that the wings of the aircraft almost touched the wire fence they nestled behind.

On exiting the fusty airport, I was met by a man holding a board with my name whose job it was to drive me to the site, three hours away. We piled into his white Ambassador car. It was 8 pm and dark by the time we arrived at the site gates and despite being told by the company I would be staying in the relative safety of the site compound, the driver had been given instructions to take me to the 'guest house' which entailed another half-hour drive to a neighbouring village. I'm sure you can imagine the horrors going through my mind as I tried to picture what a guest house in deepest Sindh province would turn out to be. The driver didn't speak any English and I was knackered after travelling all day, so little conversation passed between us en route.

Eventually we arrived at the village, a place I later learned to be Dharki. He pulled up at the side of the main road. I knew this because it was the only one with street lighting even if it was in the form of a sparse number of light bulbs draped over a wire. It was still pitch black and I had absolutely no idea where I was. At this point it appeared my driver did speak English although his grasp of the language may have begun and ended with the word 'Out', which he repeatedly shouted at me.

'What do you mean "out", where the hell are we?' I replied with sufficient gesturing to make myself understood.

He did no more than turn the car engine off and go to get my holdall out of the boot. I was now getting seriously worried, so using some hand signals I had learnt on my emergency training, I told him to 'leave the case' and 'stay where he was.'

As my eyes grew accustomed to the darkness, I could just make out what looked like a row of garages and my driver was pointing into them. Most had iron bars on the front but one had no door. I peered inside and groped my way up a set of stairs to discover a door with a light shining underneath it. Not sure who or what was lurking behind it, but by now way too tired to care, I knocked loudly. To my immense relief a man dressed in traditional Pakistani dress opened the door and greeted me with 'Ah, Mr Rayns.' It seemed Imran, who ran the guest house with his Korean wife Kim, had been expecting me. He welcomed me inside whilst shouting to the driver to bring my bag up, and fortunately for me he spoke English. There were four bedrooms, all occupied by Korean workers. There being no room at the inn, I was put up in the owners' bedroom which had the added luxury of en suite facilities – shower, basin, and a hole in the floor toilet with accompanying hand spray but no toilet paper.

Before I turned in for what was going to be a very short night's sleep, Imran and Kim, despite the late hour, rustled up some food and informed me that breakfast was served at 7 am sharp, with the car coming at 8 am to take me to site. When I went down the next morning, the Koreans had already left but Kim served up a breakfast of chips, beans and coleslaw – all cold, but I was touched by the effort she'd gone to find me some familiar food.

At five to eight, the car, an old 1950s Morris Oxford, arrived. Up front, the driver had a soldier for a passenger. I got in the back and another soldier sat next to me and then we waited. I assumed this was because we were going to leave at 8.00 am on the dot, so when the old dashboard stick-on digital clock clicked to 8.01, I took this as my cue to ask why we weren't moving.

'We are waiting for the Danger Car.'

I thought I was already in the Danger Car because the driver and I were both flanked by an armed soldier, but apparently, we had to wait for the escort. Minutes later, an old pick-up truck arrived with a machine gun mounted over the top of the cab and a soldier in protective gear clinging onto it for dear life. The Danger Car was a look-out car, its sole purpose being to look for danger and I couldn't go anywhere without it. I'm not sure if it occurred to anyone other than me that the time I might be in most danger was while sitting in the Morris Oxford waiting for the Danger Car to arrive.

A few days into my stretch, Friday, the holy day, came around so I didn't have to go to site. Breakfast, still cold, was served at a slightly more civilised 8.00 am after which I fetched my jacket and headed to the door to go for a walk. And that was as far as I got, because Imran was blocking my way, demanding to know where I was going.

'I'm going for a walk up and down the village, and as it's market day, I'll probably have a look around there too.'

'I am sorry, Mr Rayns, but the Danger Car is not available on a Friday.'

'It's OK, I don't need the Danger Car, I'm just going outside for a walk.'

He refused to let me pass and his attitude was starting to worry me. I asked him what danger could I come to on a short walk. He tactfully explained that what I didn't understand was that there were a lot of 'uneducated people' who would see my white face and therefore know that I had probably got a nice watch on my wrist and a fat wallet in my back pocket, and wouldn't think twice about..., at which point he broke off from his explanation to perform a mime of someone slitting my throat. I informed him I didn't really fancy a walk and would probably go back to my room. Suddenly the prospect of spending a day reading yet another Jeremy Clarkson Top Gear paperback seemed appealing.

My stay in deepest, darkest Pakistan lasted ten days, and thankfully I didn't see any danger, and neither did the Danger Car.

The only real trouble I had was eating my dinner. Each evening, a bell rang to call everyone to the table. When I sat down with the Korean workers one night, there was only an empty dish, a fork and a pair of serrated scissors in front of me. Kim came in carrying a huge pan which she placed in the middle of the table and then got out a large pair of forceps. Steam poured from the pot as she removed the massive lid and proceeded to extract and place in front of each expectant guest a whole, enormous, boiled crab. The Korean workers voiced their delight, I managed to keep my reaction to myself.

Now this wasn't a dish that had made it onto the menu at my local takeaway and somewhere in the back of my mind I knew there was a part of the crab that you shouldn't eat. No matter how hard I searched the recesses of my brain, I couldn't remember where in the crab it was. The Korean guys looked like they knew what they were doing so I decided to watch them and copy. They tucked in with relish, tearing off the claws, expertly loosening and extracting the meat with the scissors, sucking up the juice and spitting out the shell. I pulled off a claw and then attempted, with the dexterity of a two-year-old, to extract the meat using the scissors. Worried I might lose a finger on the next try, I made my excuses, muttering something about needing to finish my Clarkson book, and went to bed hungry.

Although the crab was impossible to eat, the award for the worst food I ever found myself in front of would be a close call between Korea and Norway. The Korean weekly site canteen menu consisted of rice and fish or fish and rice. Yes, breakfast, lunch, and dinner were all the same. Occasionally the fish was substituted by rubbery pieces of hacked-up octopus tentacle and, rarely, chicken chopped-up into

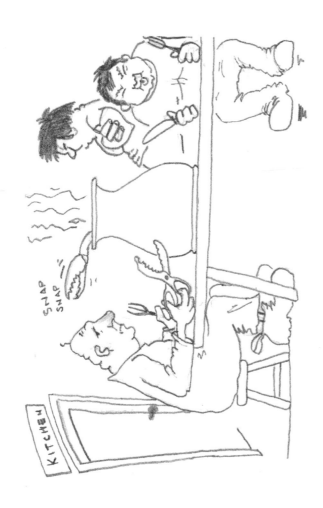

so many pieces you had no idea where your bit came from but I'm guessing, the arse end. A welcome addition to the menu was Kimchi, a traditional side-dish of salted fermented vegetables, usually cabbage and radish. It was originally stored underground in jars to keep it cool and provided a much-needed supply of vegetables during the winter months. The Korean menu also doubled as a weight-loss programme, generally about 3 kilos a week. However, the winner, by a hair's breadth, is Norway. Normally the home of exquisite cuisine, both on and offshore, somewhere in its history it has managed to create one of the most repulsive meals ever. Lutfisk is a dish of dried cod soaked in caustic soda for several days to rehydrate it and yes, that is the same caustic soda they put in oven and drain cleaner. It is supposedly rinsed well, though I have my doubts, before being boiled or baked and served with potatoes and a gravy boat full of hot bacon fat. It has a unique aroma and be warned that if you order it in a restaurant and manage to force down a plateful without gagging, it is traditional to serve it twice, so leave room for that second delicious helping.

* * * * *

In 2010 while running my own company, a German client I did a lot of subcontract work for approached me with the offer of a job in Nigeria. I declined the invitation, Nigeria being notoriously dodgy and undoubtedly one of the most corrupt countries in the world. Rather than its substantial oil reserves bringing prosperity to the country the vast majority of its population continue to live in abject poverty. It is impossible for a white-skinned person not to attract attention and the risks of being robbed and killed for your wallet and watch or kidnapped in order to extort money from your employer make travelling around without official protection extremely dangerous.

A couple of days later the big boss phoned saying he wanted me to go and see him to discuss the matter. I had no intention of going, but they were paying my expenses and day-rate, so off I went to Germany. He said, sounding almost genuinely surprised, he'd heard I'd declined the job in Nigeria. I explained my concerns but he said they were under an obligation to commission some equipment there and when they had told the client in Nigeria that they couldn't find anybody to send because of the security conditions, the client had said 'name your own price'. Tempting as this may have been, I explained I had just entered into my fifties, really wanted to see my sixties and the price of my life was not open to negotiation. From all accounts they did recruit someone to go but he bottled it after four days because he had difficulty sleeping in the secure compound, mainly because of the sound of gunfire outside.

A couple of months later, my old friend Don from Rolls-Royce in America called me. Don was from Arizona and raced lawn mowers in his spare time. Not the 12-inch Suffolk colt variety, these were ride-on ones with V8 engines. I don't know if he ever succeeded in fitting an airplane gas turbine engine on one but he certainly wanted to try. Surprise, surprise, they also had some equipment they wanted commissioning off-shore in Nigeria.

Sounding like a stuck record, I explained I was sorry but had already recently turned down one job because of the security situation. He asked me not to make a hasty decision and at least read through a copy of the security measures they had in place to look after the welfare of all their workers over there. I agreed, just to get rid of him, and a few days later a dossier of forty A4 pages arrived. There were a lot of general dos and don'ts like needing to be vaccinated against rabies and yellow fever and details of the random blood tests they imposed in areas where malaria was prevalent to ensure you had taken your quinine. I was giving the document the cursory look I thought it deserved when my attention was drawn to a photo of the guy in charge of personal security. I only glanced at his name which ended in OOKA, and from that point on I called him Mr Bazooka. He looked like he could go the distance with Mike Tyson and then carry on with his day job. The security procedure on arriving in Nigeria was not to proceed to the airport baggage claim until you had met Mr Bazooka and under no circumstances to leave the terminal building without him. You would never have to arrange your own accommodation or travel, it would all be taken care of by Mr Bazooka who had one mission – to keep you out of harm's way. I read it and reread it and decided to go, clear in my own head that if at any moment I felt uneasy I would be on the next plane back. They sent the necessary letter of invitation for me to apply for a visa from the Nigerian embassy in London and the Nigerian government sent the necessary sponsorship letter. I eventually got my visa but only after responding to a phone call from the embassy demanding I send 'more money.' Another fifty quid was sufficient.

Six weeks later I was stepping off the plane at Lagos. I went to immigration and straightaway the official looked at my paperwork and white face, clocked I had arrived to work in the country and wasn't shy to ask if I had any money for him.

'No, I'm meeting Mr Bazooka', I said.

It seemed he knew exactly who I was talking about and didn't want to get on the wrong side of him. My bag was just coming around on the carousel when Mr Bazooka arrived looking even more menacing in the flesh. Ticking my name off his list, his enormous hands making the pen look like a matchstick, he instructed me to get my bag and then wait for him before entering customs. I waited by Nothing to Declare for ten or fifteen minutes but kept him in my sights the whole time. When he came back, he said the no-show guy had bottled it and we could now go.

We stepped outside into a hot and humid afternoon. He beckoned to a big black 4 x 4 Mercedes parked nearby. I slung my bags in the boot and got in the back, grabbing the handle of the open door to pull it shut. Jeez, it was stiff. I assumed because it was new (I could smell the leather upholstery) but it relented and closed when I gave it a good hard tug. The driver and soldier got in and the armed escort pulled into position in front and we set off for the hotel. From the start, the driver was going hell for leather nose to tail with the armed escort in front. He had a huge bull horn which he had no worries about wearing out. Its constant blaring had the desired effect, the traffic in front of us parting like the Red Sea.

At this point I was starting to regret making use of the in-flight drinks trolley as each time I looked through the front windscreen I felt sick. I glanced out back and felt just as nauseous as there was another armed pick-up at the back equally as close. In desperation I looked out of the side window and it was then that I realised the reason the door was so heavy was because it was armour-plated with half-inch thick bulletproof glass windows. There was no doubt my personal safety was being taken seriously.

After half-an-hour of struggling to keep the contents of my stomach in, we arrived at the hotel.

The soldiers posted on the gate carried out some rigorous security checks before allowing me entry. Mr Bazooka lived up to my expectations and arrived the next morning to take me to the heliport.

My trip offshore was hindered because of a strike by the local oil workers who were being paid a pittance in comparison to their western counterparts. As I was pretty self-sufficient and not keen to extend my stay, I carried on working. It wasn't long before two well-built Nigerian workers approached me and asked if I knew they were on strike. When I told them I did, they said that I was by all means free to carry on working but they wouldn't be able to guarantee my safety. I thought about asking if they had met Mr Bazooka but was stopped by a strong urge to go and finish my Clarkson book. It was a relief when a month later I was escorted in one piece back to the airport.

* * * * *

Early on in my career, the words 'safety' and 'conscious' hadn't always appeared in the same sentence. I was driven by a need to pay the bills and accepted contracts in a number of dodgy, and some even dodgier, locations. Angola was definitely at the top end of the dodginess scale. The first leg of the journey was a BA flight from Heathrow to Johannesburg. From there I was to pick up a South African Airlines flight to Luanda but Johannesburg

Airport had different ideas. On presenting my visa and accompanying letter of invitation, the check-in girl informed me there was an 'anomaly'. She went off to speak to a colleague. Twenty minutes later she returned to say there was still an 'anomaly' and I wasn't going to be allowed on the flight. Apparently, a number on my passport didn't match the one shown on the letter of invitation. On my passport the digit was a '2' but on the faxed copy of the letter of invitation the 2 had become a '7'. I'm no handwriting expert, but it was obvious to me that the 7 was in fact a 2 but the bottom part had not printed-out properly. By this time, an hour had passed. The flight was about to close but I appeared to be the only one with any sense of urgency. After I'd explained my theory, she called a colleague over who suggested I ask my UK office to fax through another copy. I complied but the one that came through looked exactly the same as the one I'd presented. Next the check-in supervisor turned up. By now I had identified another '2' on the faxed copy that also looked like a '7' and pointed this out. After a lot of 'umming' and 'ahhing' they decided that it was a '2' after all. By which time the plane had taken off and I would have to get the next one, in two days' time. I asked if there were any other airlines flying to Luanda. My luck was in. Angola National Airlines had a flight the next day so I forked out for that, and stayed in the airport hotel overnight.

At this time, I was a relative novice to long-haul travelling and didn't have the contact details for the person picking me up at the other end to inform them of my new travel arrangements. After boarding the Angola airlines flight, I decided this was just as well as it was the oldest jumbo jet I had ever seen and I doubted its ability to get me to my destination. It was so antiquated it still had piped music, the original jumbo jet music system which had headphones with tubes, no cable. All the overhead lockers came open on take-off because of the vibration but by some miracle the plane survived and I landed in Luanda at 10 pm. As anticipated, there was no one to pick me up. I didn't even know which hotel my reservation was at, so I got my bag, hailed the first cab I saw, and asked for the nearest hotel. This was ten minutes away according to the driver but seemed much further as he drove through a succession of dark alleyways with me fearing for my life. He deposited me at a hotel where I was greeted with the worrying news that they were full. Wondering when Luanda had become a top tourist destination, I asked if they knew of anywhere else and after a quick phone call, I was told the Meridien had vacancies and they were expecting me. I got back into a taxi which I hoped was taking me to the next hotel and not a violent death. After another tense 20-minute drive through yet more dark alleys, I arrived.

The next day was Saturday which meant I wouldn't be going anywhere until I could make contact with my client on the Monday. The hotel staff insisted I didn't go out because being white, people would be looking to rob me, so I spent the weekend holed-up like a celebrity under house arrest. I rang my client on the Monday to discover it was a bank holiday in Germany and no one would be in the office until Tuesday.

The thing about being told you shouldn't do something is that it immediately ignites a burning desire to do just the opposite. So, after two-and-a-half days in confinement and having forgotten to pack my Clarkson book, I thought 'sod it' and left the building. It was a nice sunny day and I took a walk around the hotel but I could feel people watching me from their doorways, so a modicum of common sense prevailed and I headed back to a more public place. A few minutes from the hotel was the harbour and as I wandered around, a guy sitting on a bench asked me the time. Just as I went to say twenty-past one, I realised that the harbour clock was opposite him. He was more interested in knowing if I spoke English and asked what I was doing. I used my usual cover story of working on the air conditioning at the airport. You never admitted to anyone you were working offshore as a lot of the time the locals didn't like the fact you were getting paid from money that the average man never saw. He was a jolly big bloke and he asked if I fancied going for a beer. I thought 'why not?', and followed him along to a small bar on the corner with half a dozen tables.

I ordered a beer, he a large vodka. These slipped down nicely and we ordered another while making small talk – was I married, how much did my watch cost, did I have children, how much did my shirt cost. The increasingly surreal experience continued as some Russian sailors arrived filling up the other tables and punctuating the air with toasts of 'nazdarovya'. I drank my beer and he asked if I wanted vodka. Next thing two glasses and a bottle of vodka arrived on the table. After an hour, conscious it was starting to get dark, I thought I had better get back.

My buddy was now three-quarters of the way through though the bottle of vodka. I asked for the bill, paid the lot and legged it back to the hotel leaving my new best mate with his liquid friend. My stupidity had cost me an afternoon of free booze for my companion. I was lucky that was all.

Engineer on Fire

'Brace, brace, brace.' Now there are three words guaranteed to cause some serious arse twitching, especially if you are 120 miles out to sea onboard a helicopter at the time the pilot shouts them. Assuming you manage to escape in one piece when the chopper ditches, it won't be long, an hour at most, before the cold waters of the North Sea send you to a hypothermia-induced death. And that's with your survival suit on. Prospects aren't much better if you ditch in warmer waters. There's a reason they've replaced your survival suit with a pouch of coloured dye – it's to repel the sharks.

Undeterred by these odds, the powers that be demand all off-shore personnel complete a relevant survival course. For me it's the BOSIET or Basic Offshore Safety Induction and Emergency Training with Emergency Rebreather System. The five day course includes such fun activities as escaping from a submerged helicopter, righting a capsized life raft, basic first aid, and firefighting. The certificate lasts four years and can be updated by completing a one-day refresher course three months before its expiry date. The only thing worse than doing the Offshore Refresher Course is having to redo the whole bloody five-day course because you've been delayed on a job abroad and missed the cut-off date for the refresher. The first time I was subjected to this ordeal was in the mid-80s and it was so much fun I vowed never to do it again, as I have done every time I've had to redo it since.

HOTA in Hull was my torture chamber of choice. It's a civilised start with coffee and biscuits and a morning in the classroom running through the timetable of activities. More importantly, everyone's identity is verified though why anyone would want to send someone in their place is beyond me!

In 2008, oh deep joy, I'm back in Hull to take the full course because yet again I've missed the refresher cut-off date. Sitting next to me on day one is Billy, a Yorkshire lad, around 25 years old and well-built to say the least. When the course tutor gets to saying 'and Wednesday you will be in the dunker' the big lad turns to me and says,

'I can't wait for that, it's the bit am reet lookin' forward to.'

I know we live in an age where thrill-seeking is a national pastime, whether it's throwing yourself out of a plane or off a cliff attached to nothing more than a piece of pyjama elastic. The extreme sports of my youth consisted of sledging on an old tin tray and riding downhill on my bike with my eyes shut. The only part of the HOTA course I'm looking forward to is the end. I attempt to impart the wisdom of my years.

'Look', I say, 'I've done this course many times and the part I hate the most is the dunker. I don't mind groping my way in pitch darkness through a building filled with thick, black, acrid smoke, and flames licking at my arse, even if it is encased in a fire-retardant suit. Not my first choice for a night out, but the helicopter escape is the worst. Maybe it's me, but breathing underwater is for fishes and not what my body was designed for.'

Wednesday has come around all too quickly for my liking. After a morning in the classroom learning how to use the rebreather we're ready for the afternoon session in the dunker. We've rehearsed everything so many times we can do it blindfold – just as well as it's pitch black in the sea. The drill goes: locate nearest exit, put nearest hand on nearest exit and keep other hand free. As the helicopter submerges it rolls over and you are engulfed in a mass of bubbles. By keeping your hand on the direction of escape you avoid becoming disorientated in the dark. Well, that's the theory at any rate. The instructor yells 'Brace, brace, brace', the signal to get the hood of the survival suit out of your pocket, onto your head and then your hand back on the direction of escape. As you tear down the front panel of the rebreather, out falls the pipe with the mouthpiece, valve block, and nose clamps on it. Using your free hand, you pick up the mouthpiece, shove it in your trap, give a couple of puffs, and then put the nose clamps on. The water rises up to your neck in a matter of seconds, at which point you take a big deep breath, click the valve and breathe into the bag. Breathing in the classroom is completely different to breathing when submerged. The water pressure against the bag has the weight of a sack of potatoes and it really is an effort to force your breath out. Next, your hand goes to the four-point seat belt buckle which you turn to open once the helicopter has rolled over. These steps are practised until they can be performed with both hands. Even after the morning training session, my Yorkshire colleague is still bursting with enthusiasm, and as we go for lunch, he chimes up,

'I'm reet lookin forward to this.'

We assemble at the side of the tank, trussed up in our fetching bright yellow surival suits and red lifejacket combo with separate rebreather. The next level of training involves sitting submerged along the gantry of the tank, level with the hand rail. Frogmen in the tank check to see everyone is breathing through the rebreather. This is followed by a fifteen metre underwater swim from one side of the tank to the other, with the frogmen once again observing.

All too soon we are onto the main event and, as if escaping from a submerged helicopter once wasn't traumatic enough, you have to do it six times to pass, each time from a different seat. That's twice at the front, twice in the middle, and twice at the back where the smallest windows are, and seated on different sides of the chopper, so you use different hands. Frogmen are present, one in the helicopter and one in the tank.

My Yorkshire sidekick is in group two. I'm in group one.

'Brace, brace, brace.' I wait till the water is up to my neck and attempt to keep my biggest enemy, panic, in check. By the time I've blown into the bag I'm underwater and hanging upside down. I force the window out with my elbow, turn the buckle, fall out of my seat, pull myself out, surface, regroup and get ready to go again.

My self-inflicted ordeal is eventually over and I'm at the side, hanging up my survival suit for another four years. There's a commotion in the tank. Somebody's got stuck trying to exit out the small back window. The frogman inside the helicopter is trying to push the guy out, his hands going where the sun don't shine. The one outside is using some manoeuvres I've seen on the Yorkshire Vet on TV, you know, when a cow is giving birth to an oversized calf. He's got hold of the grab handle on the back of the would-be escapee's suit and eventually pulls him through. When the giant yellow condom-encased form surfaces, I realise it's my Yorkshire mate. He got stuck on his first attempt but all credit to him, he got back in and gained his certificate. Next morning, he was quick to tell me,

'Tha's reet, tha knows. That dunkas not rite nice was that.'

The problem of safely transporting increasingly broad-shouldered helicopter passengers did not go unnoticed by the Civil Aviation Authority, nor did they treat it lightly. In April 2015 it became a requirement for personnel travelling by helicopter to an offshore installation to submit their shoulder measurement. Anyone with a measurement of larger than 55.9 centimetres would be classed as Extra Broad (XBR) and would have to wear a black and white chequered armband and sit in a helicopter seat compatible with their shoulder size, i.e. next to the big windows which were now also chequer marked.

As the wife, who's not adverse to be bit of dressmaking when the need arises, stood poised with her freshly untangled tape measure, I had to inform her that she was not adequately qualified to perform the task in hand. It could only be carried out by a specially-trained OPITO approved medical or occupational health professional. She went off muttering something about the world going mad, and I tended to agree when I saw the £45 charge payable for the ten minute service.

* * * * *

Sometimes I wished I had a regular job with regular hours and without the need to do a safety course which, in truth, was probably going to be of little help to me if the helicopter I was in ditched in the freezing waters of the North Sea.

There are also a whole host of things you don't want to happen when you're offshore. A bout of acute appendicitis when it's too choppy for the medivac helicopter to land springs to mind. Another is someone shouting 'Fire', especially if it's you.

Some reassurance comes from that in UK, Danish, and Norwegian waters measures are in place to ensure everyone knows what to do. During the weekly boat drill, often timed for 2 am in the morning, you gather at your appointed muster station sometimes preparing to board your designated lifeboat. If the bastard in charge is really going for it, boarding the lifeboat and strapping yourself in. The lifeboat launches from a height of 75 feet at an angle of 45 degrees. The strapping is there to stop your head parting company with your neck when it hits the water. In the event of an incident occurring, an alarm is sounded. The GPA (general platform alarm) means get to your muster station, while the PAPA (prepare to abandon platform) means 'we're in some seriously deep shit. Get to your designated lifeboat and start praying'.

I was offshore Norway on a big refit along with a Norwegian colleague Knut (more about him later) and his team. This was a big job involving taking out a diverter damper, a section of the stack, and all the expansion joints, combined with a turbine engine change. The platform was on a two-week shutdown. Ten days in, things were progressing well. I was kicking my heels waiting for the cold commissioning to be finished, so took sanctuary from the freezing conditions in the accommodation block. It wasn't long before another guy joined me.

'All OK up top?' I asked.

'Yeah, just a bit of smoke off the new expansion joints when we first ran the turbine, probably because they're new.'

A silent alarm, the one in my head, started to ring and I wasted no time heading out to take a look. Smoke was issuing from the top of the stainless steel collar where the cladding terminates as it goes up the stack. An inspection of the diverter and ducting at waste heat recovery level revealed nothing. I headed down a level following the ducting. Nothing. Down another level to the turbine – and bingo! Through the glass panel of the turbine enclosure, I could see naked flames.

'Bran, bran, fire, fire' I shouted heading for the nearest emergency button. Within ten minutes of the words leaving my lips I was strapped into the lifeboat ready to launch. The fire response team were equally quick and extinguished the fire so I didn't get to test how effective the strapping is at keeping your neck attached to your head.

As usual, these situations are never down to one thing but a combination of events. The night shift had a burst hydraulic hose on some hired-in big nut splitters. With the hose replaced, work proceeded, but about twenty litres of hydraulic fluid had escaped. Normally any hydraulic equipment that goes offshore has to have fire retardant hydraulic fluid in it but this piece of hired-in kit had escaped that requirement. When the gas turbine is fired up ready for hot commissioning, some of the safety features are disabled temporarily. The spilt hydraulic fluid leaked down the duct, into the hot GT enclosure, ignited, and started to burn between the duct and the insulation. The only place the smoke could escape was at the collar of the stack. Norwegian efficiency meant the incident was dealt with promptly and effectively. If only I could have said the same when I was offshore Brazil.

I was on board an FPSO (or floating bomb). This was an oil tanker with a deck the length of two football pitches and an oil refinery plonked on the top. It was towed out to sea and once in position, anchored to the seabed where it would remain for the duration of its working life. I'd been brought in to commission the dampers and waste heat recovery units on the gas turbines and things were running seriously behind schedule. The client had also taken the decision to produce and export oil while the FPSO underwent significant commissioning.

I don't know whether it's due to environmental issues, but the flare tips, from the burning-off of any unwanted gases encountered whilst producing crude, used to overhang the sea at an angle. These were then altered so that they seem to be completely perpendicular and therefore above the deck, albeit very high. This was a big FPSO and had a big flare tip. I think there were twelve, forty-five centimetre diameter burner nozzles all contained within a forty centimetre high bund which served to retain any spillage. I was on my mid-afternoon tea break, although calling that particular mug of liquid 'tea' may have been a breach of the Trade Descriptions Act. As I was also having a chuff, I was in the designated smoking area placed behind the firewall. All of a sudden, I heard an almighty roar and people started pointing up to the flare. I had my back to it, but could tell from the noise that it had a good flame on it. A couple of minutes later the roar turned into a cough, then a splutter, and out of the flare nozzles where only waste gas should emerge, there were big blobs of crude, as big as footballs, being spat out and shot in the air. The bund was overflowing with crude which was dripping down the structure onto the deck below. As the footballs of crude landed on the deck they ignited and within minutes the bow of the vessel and the flare tips were engulfed by fire. It wasn't good, and not waiting for the GPA (General Platform Alarm) to go off, I put my cigarette out and headed to my muster station.

102

The Fire Response Team appeared, a dozen men in total, dressed in full firefighting gear. They were heading towards the bow and making as much progress as a car on the M25 during rush hour. Fire balls were raining down on the workers at the front of the boat, a couple of hundred in total, so not surprisingly they were heading down to get behind the firewall. After a couple of minutes, the process guys isolated the flare to stop any more gas or crude from going up, and eventually when the Fire Response Team did get down the fire burnt itself out as well as getting smothered with foam. The GPA never went off and as this vessel was half full of crude there could easily have been a catastrophe.

Thankfully, I have never experienced a serious disaster on or offshore but I have been called in to examine the aftermath. Some things in life go together like cheese and pickle on a sandwich, while others, like a litre and half of wine and the wife don't and should be avoided at all costs. It's not surprising then, that when someone made a decision to store a haul of confiscated gunpowder at the Evangelos Florlaks Naval base 25 kilometres from the main power station at Vasilikos, and nature intervened with a nearby bush fire, Cyprus had a problem.

A few days after the explosion, when the powers that be had got their ducks in a row, a decision was made by the unfortunate insurance company handling the claim, to call in all the necessary experts to survey their particular area of the plant and report

103

back. I got the backend, reporting on the gas turbines, waste heat recovery units, bypass diverters and bypass stacks.

I landed at ten in the evening, too late to do anything productive except head to the hotel bar for a beer. After breakfast, I made contact with the client, and the hotel concierge booked me a taxi to the plant. It was about a half-hour's drive away, but being an engineer and not a holiday rep, I had no idea in which direction. I got in the front seat and handed the driver a piece of paper with the address on.

He took one look at it, looked at me, and then sat back and said 'No.'

I looked back at him and said 'Yes.'

After a brief discussion about it not being possible because there had been an explosion and the road was closed, I convinced him that I had been invited over to survey the site and that as I was paying him, perhaps we could at least drive over there and see if we could get through.

Fifteen minutes into the journey we pulled off the main road, the remnants of a barricade visible. Half a mile further on at the crest of a hill, there was another barricade with an opening in the middle just big enough to squeeze a car through. From here we looked downhill into a huge bowl where the power plant had been situated in the middle. I was unprepared for the view I got, my eyes immediately drawn to a huge tree which had been snapped in half, the top parts leaning down at forty-five degrees. As my eyes panned around the bowl, every tree was the same. The power plant, just visible in the distance, was a scene of utter devastation as if a bomb had been dropped on it.

I spent the next three days on site carrying out my survey. Walking around, it was obvious the plant had taken the full force from a downwards blast. It had passed down the bypass stack and blown the open diverter closed. The massive gear boxes attached to either end had been smashed to pieces and the bottom of the bypass stack and the site were littered with shrapnel and 50 millimetre diameter disks. It was a catastrophic explosion, sadly not without the loss of human life, as at the time of the blast the fire department was still trying to contain the nearby forest fire.

Engineer on Four Wheels

I may be qualified and proficient in all things mechanical, but over the years I've learned never to underestimate how much trouble the humble car can be. In my day, and given the nature of my job, I've been a frequent user of hired cars.

Arranging for a hire vehicle has some things in common with online dating. What turns up on the day all too often bears no resemblance to the description and photo on the web page. Car hire companies also delight in offering cars with the latest technology and gizmos, so that it's only possible to put the handbrake on and change gear if you possess the brains of a Mensa member.

In 2010, the second wife and I set off on a business trip to Recklinghausen, an industrial town in the North Rhine-Westphalia region of Germany. Jan and I had met in a nightclub in Nottingham, our shared home town, a few months after the anti-climax of the new millennium. Either fate or too many pints of lager threw us together, probably the latter. Normally, I went for petite blonds. Jan was a tall brunette with glasses. It turned out our lives had been interwoven for some time before we met. Jan already knew my sister-in-law, Sam, and our sons had met at a school holiday club. Maybe fate was at work somewhere, after all.

I knew I'd met the woman of my dreams when she said she liked football, a prerequisite for any relationship with me. She's spent the last nineteen years protesting that her actual words were that she liked 'Fantasy Football', a TV programme presented by Frank Skinner, one of her favourite comedians and not because it had anything to do with the greatest game on earth. But I know what I heard.

We were both carrying more excess baggage than a British Airways flight would allow, so it's not surprising that over the years our relationship has been subject to bouts of turbulence. Even so, we make a good team, and when the time came in 2004 to set up my own company, despite her having a full-time job, running around after a couple of teenagers, and studying for a degree, she took on the role of company secretary, dealing with the day to day admin.

As we reached the outskirts of Recklinghausen, the last shreds of daylight disappearing, we punched the hotel address into the portable satnav.

Immediately we discovered that the task of checking that our satnav had the right maps on it hadn't fallen into the remit of either the Company Secretary or the Project Manager. OK, we did have part of Europe – but France, Spain, and Portugal – none of which were of much use to us at that point. Using our sense of direction, we navigated a path towards the centre of Recklinghausen which was when, to our great delight, we discovered it was the one night of the year that a big fireworks celebration took place. Every street we tried to turn down was blocked-off. After three circuits and still unable to locate the hotel I'd picked specially because it had a decent sized car park, I took a right instead of a left and entered a huge paved square surrounded by shops and restaurants. The wife rolled her eyes and gave me one of those 'what the f**k are you doing driving the car on here' looks. I took great delight in pointing out that there was another car on the opposite side. She took even greater delight in telling me that it was a police car. Perfect, at least we now had someone to ask for directions, a task I delegated to the wife. Their English was fractionally better than our German, and we followed them as they led us down a narrow gangway with barricade boards on one side. As we turned the corner, they indicated the hotel was on the left. Everything to the right had been demolished to make way for a shopping mall, including the hotel's carpark. We had the choice between leaving the car on what remained of the pavement and risking a fine, or finding the only other car park, which was across town. We left it where it was and headed out for a beer.

* * * * *

I had not been immune to the odd bit of car trouble earlier in my career. In the 1980s I was working in Nottingham as an Assistant Project Engineer. The title was grand but the job wasn't and when some paint needed fetching, it appeared this fell within my job description. These were the days before the Assistant Project Engineer was deemed worthy of a company car, but before I was banned from driving for being an idiot, so I was given the use of Colin Hall, the Chief Engineer's two-year-old 1.8 litre Morris Marina. Colin was a man of few words and though he was 6 foot 7 tall, he was too skinny to be imposing. All I had to do was drive the thirty minutes to the paint manufacturer at Sutton-in-Ashfield, pick up a couple of five litre cans of heat-resistant aluminium paint, and deliver them back to the office by 5 pm. What could possibly go wrong?

On the plus side, I completed tasks one and two without difficulty. As I drove back through Sutton-in-Ashfield and neighbouring Kirkby-in-Ashfield, the road climbed steeply uphill to a T-junction. The lights changed to red as I approached so I pulled up sharply cranking the handbrake on. As soon as they changed to green, I sped off down the bypass like a bat out of hell. All of a sudden there was a Ford Cortina behind me, flashing its lights. There are two things you can do when the driver behind is flashing you. One, the sensible option, is to pull over slightly and let them pass. The other is to put your foot down. Being only in my mid-twenties, I opted for the latter, forgetting I was in my boss's Morris Marina and not my everyday car, a three litre GT Capri that could go like shit off a shovel. Consequently, the car that was behind me flashing was still behind me flashing a mile further on, as another set of traffic lights on red came into view. The road split into two lanes and the other guy pulled alongside me, gave me a pip on the horn, and wound his window down. Reluctantly, I wound mine down too.

'You've got something pissing out your boot mate', he shouted. 'That's why I've been flashing you. It might be water or petrol, but you're leaving a trail.'

Humbled, I muttered thanks and pulled in as soon as I could. I had a strong suspicion it was neither water nor petrol, but I wasn't prepared for the disaster that greeted me when I opened the boot. Both cans had gone over, both lids had come off, and what remained of the ten litres of paint was now swilling around the boot. Heat resistant paint is piss-thin at the best of times. It was in both boot wells and all over the spare wheel and jack, and the boss's Barbour wax jacket.

110

Luckily there was also a paint covered shovel in there and being in the countryside I dug up a load of soil and chucked this all over the boot to soak up the paint.

I arrived back at the office at ten to five with a sense of impending doom. The Chief Engineer and I didn't have the best of relationships, especially as he'd told me I would never be a Project Engineer because I was deficient on the engineering qualification side of things, despite completing three years at night school. He was shortly going to find out my paint-fetching skills left a lot to be desired too. The voice of wisdom was on hand in the form of my direct boss, Roy Atkins. He suggested the best thing was to own up, tell Mr Hall I would clean it out overnight and give him my car keys so he could go home in my car. In the absence of a better plan this is what I did.

When I got home, I knew I was in for a long night. I suspected even Mr Wolf from Pulp Fiction would have had his work cut out with this one. My luck didn't improve when I found my dad was also home. Though generally firm but fair, his parenting methods were at times something else. As I entered my teens, he made sure I toed the line and would spring a random room search on me. On one occasion he found the obligatory packet of cigarettes I'd forgotten to hide. He sat me down with the ashtray in front of me and told me to light one up. As soon as I'd smoked that, he made me light another, followed immediately after by another. I almost made it to the end of that one before puking up. It would be good to say that since that day I've never smoked another cigarette, but all it really taught me was not to smoke three on the trot. On another occasion, my mam was dishing up Sunday dinner while dad was clearing up outside but the window was open. Through it he heard my brother Paul, 11 at the time, giving my mam some lip. Calm as anything, he picked up the wooden clothes line prop, poked it through the window, wacked my brother on the head, and then went back to what he was doing without saying a word.

In fairness to him, he never liked to see people struggle, and when I told him what had happened, omitting the part about racing, he offered to help. We shovelled a load of sand into the boot to soak up the remaining paint and then cleared it all out revealing a once black, but now grey and white, carpet. Each time we thought we'd finished we discovered another recess the silver paint had infiltrated as it had made its break for freedom. After three hours we'd done the best job we could. Cleaning up the jacket was a futile task but I went through the motions anyway.

I turned up at work the next morning to face the music, offering immediately to buy a new jacket and boot carpet. To my surprise, Mr Hall was in a very agreeable mood.

'Come on, let's go have a look', he said, with what could have been a smile on his face, but I was afraid it might have been indigestion or wind.

After a few tense minutes while he carried out his inspection, he looked up and said,

'Well, you'd better go and fetch some more paint, but for Pete's sake take your own car this time.'

The speedo barely touched fifty all the way there and back.

A few months later disaster struck again and I was convicted of being drunk in charge of a vehicle. I'd been to the pub with some mates and despite being well over the limit, stupidly headed home in my car. Mid-journey, I got a puncture and had no choice but to pull over. I don't know how many pints I'd had but I struggled to remain upright as I extracted the spare from the boot. It was at this point the Old Bill pulled in behind me to see what I was doing.

'Officer', I slurred, 'I'm going to change this tyre and drive home.'

He threw me a lifeline and asked me again what I was going to do.

It would have been so easy to say 'I'm going to walk home and come back and sort out the flat tyre tomorrow.' But I'd had a skinful, I was invincible, and not listening to anybody.

A night in the cells had a sobering effect and when my case was heard on January 1st, a day yet to be given bank holiday status, I was banned from driving for six months. I wasn't flavour of the month with the Managing Director at the time. As I reluctantly made my way into work I was dreading having to tell him I had lost my licence as I was sure he'd take this as his opportunity to dismiss me. At Robert Mellors School I'd learnt – as I've said already – that sometimes in life you don't get what you deserve and that was certainly the case on this day. When I arrived at the office there was no sign of the Managing Director. The story I heard was he'd had a barney with his Mrs, hit the booze, crashed his car and the police had been called. He was over the limit, probably the result of drinking the other half of the bottle of Cointreau which was lying on the front seat. The company sent him on gardening leave and the Chief Engineer was put in charge. He agreed I could stay, and when I got my licence back, I was sent on my first major assignment, supervising an upgrade at a local power station.

Engineer in the Wild

You can easily come to grief at the hands, or rather the claws and teeth, of the local wildlife as I found out in the summer of 2010. I was half-way through a final six-week stretch commissioning some diverter dampers at a new oil refinery in Jamnagar, India. Loop checks had to be performed on the many cables running between the instrumentation, hydraulic power unit and the PLC (Programmable Logic Control). The gas turbines were General Electric Frame 9s, huge buggers, the biggest available. I was working as part of a team of eight, a 50/50 mix of local and foreign labour, each member doing their specialised bit of the job. The end-user, Reliance, was a massive Indian company who looked after their workers well, routinely building townships next to the refineries they were constructing. They provided everything the workers needed, including detached houses, apartments, gardens, recreational facilities, a shopping mall, medical centre, and a hospital. Thousands of Indian workers lived there enjoying cheap accommodation and a ten-minute commute to work. Being a foreigner, I was staying at a nearby hotel, but the township restaurant served a mean Chana Chaat and I regularly ate there at lunchtime.

Thursday night came around, and after a few drinks in the hotel bar, I turned-in feeling fine. At 3 am it was a different story. I woke up shivering. The air conditioning was running, a habit of mine even if the daytime temperature of 50°C dropped to a cosy 30°C overnight. I switched it off, cocooned myself in the obligatory fluffy light-blue emergency blanket from the wardrobe and slept through. The effort to hoist my body out of bed when the alarm went off at 5.30 am was horrific. I ventured into the bathroom feeling decidedly grim and ran the shower, but I was so cold I couldn't face stripping-off and donned trousers and a jumper instead. On automatic pilot I headed down for breakfast but a wave of nausea hit me and breakfast went the same way as the shower. I diagnosed a bout of flu, not man flu, real flu, so when I turned up to meet my colleagues in the lobby, I told them I was in no state to go to site and would be heading back to bed. The lead engineer was a young, skinny, Indian guy named Ravi. He didn't like the way I looked at all and despite my protests informed me he would be sending the driver back to take me to the medical centre in the Reliance township. All the drivers had instructions to pick up

foreign workers with the engine running and air conditioning on full-blast at all times. Climbing into the car, it felt like I had arrived at the Arctic Circle, so I leaned across and switched off the air conditioning, much to the driver's dismay.

Before entering the doctor's surgery, I had to take off my shoes and put on a pair of flimsy cloth slippers. To this day I have no idea why. There was a bit of a queue but it wasn't long before I was called through to be greeted by a middle-aged smartly-dressed man sitting behind a wooden desk. His medical bag was on one side, the mandatory collection of rubber stamps for all the paperwork in triplicate on the other. He was certainly thorough, questioning and then examining me before ordering blood tests and urine analysis. What he said next came as a bit of a shock. He was giving me a prescription now because I was displaying all the symptoms of malaria, and the sooner I started the medication the better. At this point nothing would have given me greater pleasure than to ask him if he was sure because I had been taking my anti-malaria medication. Only I hadn't. Back in the 1990s when I first went to work in India, I started taking quinine tablets as required the month before I was due to leave. They made me feel and look so ill that I made an informed decision not to bother, based on the fact the area I was going to was pretty low risk. When I took this latest job in India and was again prescribed quinine tablets, I made another informed decision based on the fact I'd worked in India for eighteen months without any problem and I'd only be there for a total of eighteen weeks this time. It's probably because of idiots like me, that random testing has been brought in by many employers to check that workers are taking their quinine.

I left clutching a sample bottle and headed to the toilet, passing through an empty ward, the beds regimentally placed six to each side. Despite the new and clean surroundings my eyes were drawn to the stained bedclothes. The toilet was swimming in water, at least I hoped it was water as my temporary footwear had already soaked up a fair amount. I stood discreetly behind the door to fill my pot before shuffling my wet soggy feet round to the exit, stopping off at the pharmacy for my high-dose quinine tablets. Back at the hotel I grabbed a few hours' kip.

At 2 pm the driver picked me up to take me back to the Clinic to get my test results. They had come back negative for malaria but my platelet count was very low and the doctor trusted his earlier diagnosis. He said he wanted to admit me. I didn't like to tell him I had seen the ward and there was no way I was stopping there, so I assured him I was only a short drive away at the hotel and needed to be on hand in case my work colleagues phoned for advice. On top of taking two horse tablets three times a day, he also prescribed a course of three injections in order to get even more quinine into my system quickly. As the surgery was closed on Sunday this would mean one today and two on Saturday. A blood test the following day confirmed the doctor's diagnosis of malaria. I was grateful to him for his swift intervention but also to Ravi who had insisted I go to the medical centre as the longer malaria is left untreated, the more life threatening it is. At my Monday check-up I was improving and by Wednesday I made it back to work. Dressed in overalls and armed with a tool bag I started walking over to the GT Unit I was working on some 300 metres away but had to stop halfway to hang onto a fence because I was so dizzy. My recovery was obviously going to take a bit longer.

* * * * *

I even came to grief in the exotic location of Barbados. The German company I subcontracted for had an annoying habit of offering me work in some desirable location, such as Australia or America, and then once I had confirmed my availability, emailing me to say someone else was now going on that job but there was another one in Pakistan or Angola that I could do instead. I still thought I was dreaming when not only did I get offered a job in Barbados but it wasn't substituted for a trip to Nigeria just before my departure. It was a short visit to the Arawak Cement Plant to rectify some problems they had with their dampers. I felt like a tourist as I made my way through the lush green walkway, overhung with palm trees, which led to my accommodation, a holiday apartment near St Lucy on the North-West Coast of

Barbados. This was a quiet fishing village, set on the water's edge, and opposite was the Fish Pot Restaurant which was built on the site of a seventeenth century fort and served an amazing array of local cuisine – grilled spice-rubbed tuna steak, chilled crayfish platter, parmesan fried calamari, to name a few.

I decided that after I finished the job, I'd take a few days holiday to see the south of the island and recharge my batteries. My Caribbean dream was short-lived when I developed an allergic reaction to the bites of sand-flies, so-called because they're smaller than a grain of sand and not, as their name suggests, found in sand which would give you some chance of avoiding the pesky blighters. On my last day on the job I hurried back to the apartment, brought my flight forward to that evening and arrived home looking like a kid with chickenpox.

* * * * *

During my eighteen-month contract in India in the 1990s, working on the refit of a gas-fired power station, I came up against a much larger example of the local 'wildlife'. I was based in the Fabrication Facility, a big new office purpose-built for the westerners to occupy during the execution of the project. Flimsy wooden partitions split the oblong room into four cubicles and, by Indian standards, it was nicely decorated and more importantly, air conditioned. It housed me as Project Manager, the two Bruces, and my gambling partner, Bob Plummer. Bob had the cubicle at the furthest end of the office next to the air conditioning unit which was a hole in the wall with the AC unit poking through it.

All was going well until I arrived one morning to find we had a security issue. Bob was convinced somebody had gained access to the office overnight because they had spilt coffee on the printer. Being the 1990s, this was a horizontal sheet printer and sure enough there was a coffee stain on the top sheet. Nothing appeared to have been taken, and I was mystified because the only people who had a key to the office were me and the owner and I was pretty sure he wasn't coming in to drink our coffee.

Next morning it wasn't long before shouts of 'Bastard' were coming from Bob's work area. And again there was coffee all over the sheet feeder.

'Look', he said, 'there's definitely somebody getting in here.'

' Nah. It's not possible', I said, trying to pacify him.

He dipped his finger into the pool of coffee and tasted it.

'It's coffee. Somebody's vandalising my sheet feeder. Have a taste of this', he said, dipping his finger in it again and thrusting it in front of my face.

'OK, OK, I believe you', I said, not sure where his finger had been in the hours previously.

He put the drops on his tongue to reiterate his point. 'I'm telling you, its coffee.'

It was a mystery to me as to who would be coming into the office and hardly a case of industrial sabotage, but to appease Bob, I went to see Rajesh the owner's son. Rajesh was in his late 20s and blessed with both the looks of a Bollywood actor and a quick mind. I asked him if anyone else had a key, but he reassured me that the locks had only come with two keys and we were the ones that had them.

It wasn't long before the culprit was discovered. I opened the door next morning to hear the scurrying sound of guilty feet, followed by a glimpse of probably the most enormous rat I'd ever seen in my life coming out of the end cubicle and then scuttling straight up the wire which powered the AC unit before disappearing through a gap in the wall where the unit poked through. Sure enough, the top sheet of the printer had the now familiar deposit of coffee. It all made sense. The rat was sitting on the sheet feeder so it could lean into the mug and drink the dregs of the coffee and then it weed sitting on top of the feeder. It then dawned on me that either rat piss tastes of coffee, or Bob's taste buds were not the sharpest.

While I set off to find out where our unwanted house guest was holed-up so I could serve him with an eviction notice, Bob was outside puking-up thinking of all the rat piss he'd been tasting. My investigation took me to the other side of the office wall which was in the works. A mountain of ceramic fibre insulation, a metre each in diameter, which we were using to line the inside of the ducts, was leaning against it. It wasn't feasible to move the thousands of rolls, so on my next visit to the South Extension shopping area I went on the hunt for a big rat trap. I couldn't find one that you bait and then the trap comes down and it's 'goodnight rodent' – the best I could get was a humane one.

Back at the office we baited the trap with some left-over lunch, and voilà next morning there was a rat, as big as a small cat, in the trap and trying desperately to get out.

I said, 'It's your rat Bob, you can do whatever you want with him.'

Outside the office on the opposite side of the drive was a storm culvert which always had water in it, green during the summer and black during the monsoon season. Bob dutifully got a long piece of string which he attached to one end of the rat trap, went to the storm culvert, dangled it in and eventually after a much longer time than he had anticipated the rat drowned and he brought it back up, opened the cage, and chucked the rat in the bottom of the hedge. Thinking there might well be more than one culprit, he brought the trap back in and baited it again.

Next morning, we'd caught another one. Bob told me it was my turn to do the honours so I attached the piece of string to the trap again and went over to the culvert to repeat the ritual. I was on the main thoroughfare as people were coming into work and as I was dangling the trap, I started to draw quite a crowd. An elderly guy ventured over to ask what the strange westerner was doing, so I told him we had just caught another rat in the office and I was killing it. Wagging his finger, he told me I was 'a very bad man.'

Half an hour later the internal phone rang and the factory owner asked me to go up and see him. I was a little concerned, as his son ran the factory and for Sham himself to ask to see me was unusual. He was an extremely nice man with a Gandhi-like demeanour and never had a bad word to say about anybody. Sitting opposite him, he told me he had had a complaint about me – which took me by surprise.

'One of the men in the works has seen you drowning a rat.'

I explained our problem with rats in the office and that we hadn't mentioned it, as we thought we would take care of it ourselves.

'We've caught two so far', I told him, triumphantly. 'Bob killed one yesterday and I've killed one this morning.'

'Yes, you've been seen doing it. That is why we have had a complaint. I am asking you to stop.'

I opened my mouth to protest. I didn't want to get into the detail of bubonic plague, but rats in your workspace weren't on. Religious education at our school had been basic, and learning about the world's other religions as part of the curriculum hadn't even been thought of. He explained to me that the majority of people working at the site were Hindus and Hindus believed in reincarnation.

'They don't see it as you are killing a rat; they believe you are killing a person.'

It then dawned on me why I'd only been able to find a humane rat trap in the market. I gave him my assurance we would stop and I went down to the guys and explained the situation. Before we left that night, we washed all the cups, locked up the fridge, and blocked every last hole up around the air conditioning unit.

* * * * *

In 2003, I was sent at short notice to a power plant in Egypt, two hours' drive from Cairo. I had worked at the site before, but this was to be a short three-day visit which would not overrun, at least this was the assurance I'd given the wife, who was no doubt busy packing for our holiday in four days' time. The client was a Spanish guy named Pablo who picked me up at the hotel to drive me to site. The diverter damper there was operated by a huge electric actuator and gearbox but kept tripping on torque overload causing the gas turbine to shut down and as it was the only turbine on the plant, millions of people were now without power. Needless to say, there was a real sense of urgency to get the turbine up and running again quickly, and while I could appreciate that the lack of power may be causing the people of Egypt some distress, it was nothing compared to the grief I would get if I didn't make it back to the UK in time for our holiday.

Negotiating our way out of Cairo was a challenge, and I was glad we didn't need to stop at one of the massive petrol queues with people pushing their thirsty cars into them. Egypt was, and still is, a poor country and you never knew when the filling stations were going to have petrol or diesel in their pumps. When supplies did arrive, word travelled faster than a babysitter's boyfriend when the parent's car pulls up.

Our trip to site took us out of Cairo into the barren desert, the monotony of the scenery being broken by the occasional small village or couple of camels. Eventually, we arrived in the middle of nowhere and I met the handful of people at the power plant and then got stuck into the job. At the end of the day, I extracted myself from my sweat-soaked overalls, socks, and boots and left them in the Engineer's Office along with my hard hat ready for the next day.

On our second trip to site we weren't so lucky and got stuck in a massive queue at a filling station so we were half an hour late. Everyone was waiting for me to arrive before they would do anything. Conscious that I was late and that a normal working day on the site was a demanding nine till three, with an hour and a half for lunch, it was with some sense of urgency that I rushed into the Engineer's Office where I had left my clothes. As I was busy putting everything on, the Chief Engineer was running through the list of what still needed to be done and my mind began to work out the best way to tell the wife I wouldn't be back in time, so I didn't do what I normally do ninety-nine times out of a hundred – give my boot a good shake before I put my foot in it just in case there was a venomous spider or a scorpion enjoying a lie-in. My left foot got so far in and wouldn't go any further even though I was carrying out some manoeuvres Cinderella's Ugly Sisters would have been proud of. Admitting defeat, I picked the boot up to have a close look in it. Coupled with the fact that it was a poorly lit office under a fluorescent light on a standby generator, and that due to age, between knee to foot distance I am virtually blind, to my relief I could see what I took to be a brown sock inside. As I put my hand in to pull it out, the sock moved and when I peered inside two eyes were staring up at me. I turned it upside down, shook it hard, and a rat fell out. He had pissed in my boot soaking the lining and I think I heard him say, 'That'll teach you for drowning my uncle' as he scurried away.

I must admit I had been a bit more rat-friendly when I first arrived in India and was staying at the Ashok Hotel, a Government-run hotel in Delhi. It had a pool, restaurant and five-star rating, though that perhaps should have been rat-ting. The marble bathroom had a walk-in shower, the drain for which was a three-inch diameter hole in the corner with no cover. While I was having a good hose down, every now and then out of the corner of my eye I saw something move. It seemed I had a roommate, a brown rat who was living in the drain hole. He was shy at first only popping his head up when he thought I wasn't looking and bobbing back down as soon as I caught his eye. It turned out he was having some difficulties ordering room service, so each morning I brought him up a bit of stuffed paratha from breakfast, placing a few crumbs beside the drain hole which were gratefully received. Unfortunately, the hygiene standards at the Ashok soon got the better of me. The number of food trays left uncollected for hours outside the rooms attracted a growing army of rats, but the last straw was when I was sitting in the restaurant and saw one of the waiters picking his nose. Time to move on.

Engineer on the Piste

No matter how gregarious and sociable you are, you're not going to make many good friends when your life means performing contracts – most of them relatively short – all over the world. And even if one or two work mates or colleagues on a job become more than just acquaintances, time and distance make it unlikely the friendship will last. I normally used to fall-in with the other expat lads on site and then bid them goodbye at the end of the job, not even going through the sham of saying 'Let's keep in touch.'

One happy exception is my friendship with a Norwegian engineer named Knut Klever (say it the same as in meat cleaver). Our paths first crossed in the late 1990s when he was giving a joint presentation with my then boss, Ron Sherman. They were introduced as Mr Sureman and Mr Clever and the client, probably deciding he didn't want to do business with a pair of smart Alecs, awarded the contract to their competitors.

Knut was some fifteen years younger than me and a self-confessed workaholic. What drew us together was our shared attention to detail. As I got to know him better, I suspected more than just an element of OCD (Obsessive-Compulsive Disorder). Otherwise, who would go to the trouble of moving a light fitting three inches to the right so it's in the centre of the table rather than move the table and have it slightly off-centre? On a job in Rakkestad supervising the installation of some new ducting the Korean workers had got to the stage of putting on the external insulation and cladding. A laborious job, drilling a hole and putting in a pop rivet as one piece is joined to another. It wasn't long before Knut noticed that the first ones they had put in were not in a dead straight line. In fairness to him they weren't even in any sort of line. By the time another four or five had gone in, his OCD was in overdrive. He bellowed at them.

'You've got to get them in a straight line.'

The Koreans threw him puzzled looks. Telling them to watch and learn, he demonstrated first marking a straight line and then drilling three holes along the line.

'Look, that's how I want it. All along a straight line.' And he handed back the drill and pop riveter.

All he heard for the rest of the afternoon was the buzz of the drill followed by shouts of 'slait line, slait line.' It was music to his ears.

Our friendship faltered slightly when I turned up to meet him in a hotel bar only to be greeted by the words, 'Hello, Shithead!' Knut had a great love and aptitude for languages. He didn't just speak English fluently, he'd also mastered cockney rhyming slang. Weeks earlier, I'd emailed him, starting with the affectionate greeting 'Hello Mucker'. Unfortunately, I didn't check the translation which I now know to mean 'shithead' in Norwegian.

We regularly worked on joint projects in the Norwegian sector, always finding time at the end of a job for a bit of R & R. Being Norway, this was never cheap, but the visit to Bar 1 in Oslo had me wincing for longer than normal. This establishment for the well-heeled, situated in the fashionable Aker Brygge, boasts a stock of more than 300 of the best cognacs in the country as well as whiskies and cigars though I gather stocks of the latter have diminished since the smoking ban came in.

In his best sales patter, the barman was telling us how good the old cognacs were, some of which predate the French vineyards being wiped out by Phylloxera in the mid-nineteenth century. We settled for something at the cheaper end, only fifty quid a measure. Knut declared it to be 'top notch.' It left a bitter tang in my throat, probably because I was still choking on the price, but improved a bit when Knut suggested I add a couple of hours overtime to my invoice to cover the cost.

We spent a lot of time in Bergen, a great city when it isn't raining – which being surrounded by seven mountains, it usually is – 230 days a year on average. It's buzzing during the summer months when the huge cruise liners dock and tourists descend for a stint on the terra firma. Out of season, it's hard to find anywhere with enough people to create an atmosphere. After several drunken nights in Bergen, Knut invited the wife and I to spend a weekend at a ski lodge near Lillehammer. We were relieved that the minus 32°C we experienced when we stopped for provisions en route had risen to a cosy minus 15° by the time we arrived. The trip up there was an experience. If that had been the UK, all means of transport would long since have ground to a halt. In Norway, life goes on. Snow chains have long been abandoned, the locals driving on winter tyres and nerves of steel.

The lodge was picture perfect, nestled in the snow-covered mountains with huge fir trees dotted around. There was a cosy log-burner, which was only for show, the underfloor heating being activated remotely so it was already warm when we arrived. Knut prepared us a traditional Norwegian lunch of *Rakfisk*, fermented fish, washed down with several shots of Aquavit and beer chasers.

Aquavit is the Norwegian spirit of choice, probably because at 40% proof it's guaranteed to get you hammered in no time at all. For those fortunate enough not to have tasted it, the best description is an aniseed, Pernod-type, flavour mixed with something cheap you would use to start a bonfire with or clean your paint brushes in. To sustain minimum damage, it is best necked as quickly as possible as this leaves only the five-minute afterburn where it touches the sides of your throat. When Knut and I were at the informal business acquaintance stage he offered me a drink of this legal poison. Being a Brit, and not wanting to cause offence, I did a sterling impression of actually liking the stuff. Had I known that the occasional shot was going to graduate to sessions of drinking the stuff, I would have feigned an allergic reaction.

At the end of our meal, Knut suggested we try a spot of cross-country skiing. I need to point out that before this, our experience of winter sports had consisted of some sledging in the local park with our kids but, hey, we'd had half a bottle of Aquavit, how hard could it be? We managed to ski along the snow-covered track leading from the lodge, negotiating a few small inclines even if we looked like Bambi on ice sliding down the other side. We both fell numerous times but were oblivious to the pain, every last nerve receptor having been annihilated by the Aquavit.

In the evening we tucked into another delicious meal (moose steak, killed and butchered by Knut on one of his many hunting trips) after which he asked if we'd like to go and try some proper skiing the next morning on the slopes at Hafjell. There is something about being a Brit abroad that suddenly makes you feel you have acquired the invincibility of a superhero, or Bruce Willis in *Die Hard*. The answer to this question should have been 'no way' but instead, the Brit abroad comes out with, 'Yeah, great. What time are we going?' This 'Brit abroad' madness is immeasurably enhanced if you have spent the whole day drinking beer and Aquavit, followed by several bottles of wine and a couple of large XO cognacs.

At ten next morning we were perched at the top of the 'teddy bear' slope, stone-cold sober and struggling to remain upright. All credit to the wife, who, despite being athletically challenged at the best of times, gave it a go, stop-starting all the way down. By the time she'd negotiated the chairlift and re-joined me at the top, I'm feeling more Bruce Forsythe than Willis, an old footballing injury is starting to remind me it's there and I'm wondering what the exclusion clauses on the travel insurance are. My arse has also developed an uncomfortable twitch, so I do what any husband worth his weight in gold does in these situations, I bottle it, and in the same breath suggest that Knut takes Jan for another go. Jan did what all women do in these situations and got on with it. I was gobsmacked when I watched her start off, picking up a bit of speed before disappearing out of view.

137

When she came back, resisting the temptation to say 'didn't she do well', I piled-on the praise and remarked to Knut how Jan was starting to get the hang of this. They fell about laughing. As she disappeared round the bend the speed had really picked up. After screaming at anyone in her path to get out of the way, she lost control and careered into a tree which had the desired effect of stopping her dead without breaking any bones. Her feet, with both skis still attached, were buried in three foot of snow which Knut had to dig her out of before hauling her to her feet (no mean task I can tell you). In my excitement, I'd failed to observe the tree debris in her hair and scratches on her face. We left Knut to it and headed for some après ski.

Our next get together was a more sedate affair. We nipped over the border to Sweden for some lunch and then spent the evening sabring the tops off champagne bottles with a carving knife, but Knut still remains No 1 on the wife's list of 'friends most likely to get us killed.'

Engineer at Large

Wherever I go I never forget to pack my sense of humour. It's got me through many a tricky situation. I've also never outgrown my childhood love of playing pranks. As with so many things, it's better if you have a partner in crime, so in 1984 I formed a double act with Les Charles. He was a new arrival at Becorit. We were both married, in our late twenties and liked a few beers. More importantly, we both loved football and were ardent Nottingham Forest fans. Les played for a Sunday side called Park Albion, so it wasn't long before I joined too, though the manager allocated me a permanent seat on the bench. Les was their goalie and a pretty decent one at that, but he never lived down the time he got chipped from the halfway line, the ball flying over his head and into the net while he was off his line. He was soon rechristened 'Spud' by his team mates.

After our early years together, our careers took us in different directions but converged at regular intervals. Whenever we were reunited it wasn't long before we were up to our old tricks. We never tired of subjecting our workmates to things like Cling Film™ across the toilet seat, or adding extra hot chilli sauce to a packed lunch. I mean, why would you?

In 1998 we were both working in the UK office of a German company. Like many a qualified draughtsman, Les has a certain amount of artistic talent and frankly drawing dampers all day was not stretching his creative abilities. Not a problem. He soon found another outlet, drawing caricatures of staff members, predominantly me. I'd like to describe myself as being of average height and bearing an uncanny resemblance to Brad Pitt. Unfortunately, neither are true. Being vertically challenged is not without its advantages when working in small confined spaces. Where it does create a problem is finding a pair of off-the-peg overalls that don't need a three-foot turn-up. I also had a full head of hair (in the 1970s) which I began shaving off completely in 1997 when what was left of it added insult to injury and turned white. These alone, provided ample fodder for Les to ridicule me in his sketches.

On a business trip to Norway in 1999 I needed some documents faxing over. Email had yet to be invented. I rang Les and gave him the hotel's fax number and, as the fax machine was in reception, it made sense to wait in the bar while forcing down a beer. It wasn't long before the receptionist approached me with a pile of papers smirking.

TO : MR TONY RAYNS - ROOM 216
DEPT :
FAX :
DATE: 27th SEPT 2000
FROM : LES CHARLES
COMPANY: PDS

POWER
DAMPER
SYSTEMS

TELEFAX MESSAGE

BRANCH OFFICE
BLAH, BLAH, BLAH.

HE LOOKS LIKE THIS
AND WILL BE STOOD IN
THE BAR

I took it as payback. I'd subjected him to some blinders over the years. In the early days at Becorit, the tedium of office life was getting to me and I was overcome by an uncontrollable urge to wind-up Les. I made a call to him in the Drawings Office via the internal switchboard, introducing myself as Sergeant Lomax from the local Sherwood Constabulary.

'Good afternoon. Am I speaking to Mr Leslie Charles?'

'Yes.'

'Can you confirm you are the registered keeper of a Ford Cortina, registration number ANX 10P?'

'Yes.'

'I've had a report of your car being seen in the Forest Road area of Nottingham between ten pm and midnight last week, acting in a strange manner commonly known as kerb-crawling.'

'Absolutely not. Kerb-crawling. Absolutely not.'

'Please don't get irate, sir. Perhaps you could come down to the station at five-thirty this evening to discuss the matter further. If that's not convenient we can arrange to visit you at home.'

After a round of stuttering he said, 'Can you just hold on a minute, please.'

I heard the phone being put down on the desk. He was no doubt on his way round to my office. I'd cut him off if I put the receiver down so I got Andy, my office mate, to tell Les I was on the phone to a client and out of the office fetching a file, while I hid under the desk. Sure enough, Les's size 9s shortly came

142

into view. Andy delivered an Oscar-worthy performance and I sat myself back at my desk ready to carry on the charade when Les had returned to the Drawing Office.

'Sorry about that. Yes, I'll come to the station at five-thirty.'

'Thanks for your cooperation, Mr Charles.'

I gave it half an hour and then headed down to the Drawing Office to see him squirm. He was nowhere to be seen, unlike his jacket which was draped over his chair. Never one to pass up an opportunity, I removed his car keys, went to the carpark and moved his car to the first floor of another one across the road, parking it well out of view. There was still no sign of Les when I got back, so I slipped his keys back and went on my way. The day was just getting better and better.

I could hardly wait for five o'clock and the end of the working day to come. As soon as I saw him leave, I followed him out, sauntering across the company car park from where I had a good view of him pacing up and down the adjacent municipal car park looking more and more agitated.

'What's up', I asked him.

'I can't find my f**king car. I could've sworn I parked it here this morning.'

'Well, maybe you left it somewhere else.'

'No, I always park it in this carpark and I always park it here', he said, standing in the empty space.

I wander up and down a few times, pretending to join in the search.

'Some bastard's pinched it.'

'Look, Les, if you're sure you parked it here this morning and it definitely isn't here now, then you're probably right. You'd better go down to the police station and report it stolen.'

After some hesitation and with the colour draining from his previously reddened face, he said. 'I can't. It's not taxed or insured.'

I stifled a snigger, then offered him a lift home – at which point he told me he wasn't heading home.

'Where're you going? I can probably still take you.'

He levelled with me. 'This is a f**king nightmare, this is. I've got to go to the Sherwood Constabulary because there's been a report of my car kerb-crawling.'

'Well, look on the bright side, Les, while you're there you can report your car stolen.'

I couldn't keep the masquerade up any longer. I told him where his car was and offered to sort things out with Sergeant Lomax. Retribution was only a few days away. He stuffed my car full of smoked fish. It stank to high heaven but I wound down all the windows and managed to drive out the carpark looking like nothing was amiss. Despite cleaning it out, the foul stench lingered on for several days until I found the one he'd put in the air intake for the ventilation.

Things went full circle when Les got his next car. One he wished every day would disappear. The Cortina had been condemned as not being roadworthy, and being short of ready cash he'd bought a cheap runaround. It was an in your face bright orange Skoda Rapide with black stripes. Whenever he went football training or to the pub afterwards, he parked it several streets away to avoid being the butt of the Skoda jokes of an entire football team. He upgraded to a Triumph Dolomite as soon as he could.

I wasn't the only one who enjoyed playing pranks on Les, others were queuing up. After five years at Becorit I was his line manager. We'd spent a recent evening in the pub discussing the benefits of having a vasectomy, so I wasn't surprised when he turned up in my office one Friday clutching a letter from the hospital and asking me if he could have the following Monday to Wednesday off. What I wasn't expecting was for him to reappear on the Monday afternoon.

'What's happened now, Les?'

'Well I turned up at the ward as per the letter, having carried out all the instructions. My freshly delivered sperm sample was in its plastic pot under my armpit to keep it warm and I'd done a very neat job shaving round the meat and two veg. I got stripped off and put on the green gown and then took a seat in the waiting room. I was the only guy there at this point.'

'So what was the problem? You didn't bottle it did you?'

'No. After half an hour I'm still waiting, so I go up to the reception desk and ask what's happening. The dragon there gives me short shrift, but assures me it won't be long before I'm called. After another twenty minutes, the doctor arrives. He asks me if I know Callum Peters, and then says,

'You've been had, mate. Oh, and by the way, this is the gynae ward.'

'Let me look at that letter again.' I scrutinised it closely. It certainly looked genuine, but perhaps the appointment date of April 1st should have set alarm bells ringing.

Les, when he's comatose, is an easy target. Whenever we've worked away offshore, I've always put in a request not to share a cabin with him on the grounds of health and safety, he snores like a foghorn. After some vino he's notorious for falling into a very deep sleep. Always good fun to paint his nails red when this happens and then make sure all the nail varnish remover has disappeared when he notices it the next morning.

Even recently, Les has come a cropper without anybody's help but his own. He'd moved into a new house in the spring shortly before heading off abroad on a two-month contract. Four weeks in, and one of his lads rings to say he's got a bit of bad news.

Being a bloke, Les hadn't bothered to clear the fridge out before leaving. Well, he was only going to be away for two months anyway. The electric was on a card meter and he hadn't thought to top that up either. He'd said an occasional hello to Bill and Sue who lived next door, but they had no idea he worked abroad. It wasn't long before the electric ran out and his fridge-freezer stopped working. About the same time Sue started to get a bit concerned that she hadn't seen Les for a while and popped round the back to take a look through a window. There was no sign of Les but she did see a lot of flies. Fearing the worst, she called the police, who forced the patio door off its runners to gain entry. There was no sign of a rotting corpse – just the remains of some out of date stilton and a packet of decomposing fish fingers.

I was just glad he wasn't around when I had a run-in at the gym. In an unsuccessful effort to keep trim, the second wife and I joined a local private leisure club. It was situated in a converted Victorian pumping station – the old beam engine replaced by a pool, but all the old ornate fittings had been retained. Being quite a small outfit, it didn't attract any serious bodybuilders and at some times of the day you could have the place to yourself.

I'd reluctantly turned up with the wife one Sunday afternoon, aiming to do an hour in the gym before going down the easy end for a sauna and soak in the Jacuzzi. My mood improved dramatically when I found that live football was on, Everton versus Liverpool. The wife elicited one of her 'not again' groans before sticking her headphones in. Stepping onto my treadmill of choice, I set the TV in front of me to the footy. Running can be incredibly boring, but put a ball in front of me and I can run all day. Watching the game while running was the next best thing. Out of the corner of my eye I could see the wife on one of the rowers, but I soon forgot about her, as I got into the game.

It was midway through the first half and end-to-end stuff, both teams going for it in front of a vocal full-house. Everton broke down the left wing, Liverpool were stretched. The winger ran down the pitch at full speed, the full back in hot pursuit. He delivered a perfect cross into the penalty area but there was no one there to meet it, except ME. I leapt into the air to attack the ball, climbing faster than a homesick angel, and delivered the perfect header. Direction, power, it had everything. GOAL!

Next thing I knew, I'd landed on my arse. Nothing unusual for me during a game. Dazed, I lay there looking up at the sky but it'd been replaced by a recessed ceiling light. Eventually, I heard the cheer of the crowd or could it be the wife and gym instructor laughing. The only real damage I sustained when the treadmill threw me off was a large dent to my pride but I gave it a wide berth after that.

Engineer in the Looking Glass

The day is now fast approaching when I will be hanging up my specially shortened bright orange overalls for the last time and watching with satisfaction as my HOTA certificate disappears through the shredder. Back in 1971, during my final year at school I didn't have a career plan, just a burning desire to leave at the earliest opportunity. I liked metalwork and had an aptitude for technical drawing and maths. Something to do with making stuff seemed the way to go and Raleigh bikes was the obvious choice for a Nottingham lad like me. Had I not got bored by the repetitiousness of it all, it's probably where I'd have remained until the factory closed in 2002.

Climbing the engineering ladder has been tough at times but a combination of determination, hard work, and good fortune has propelled me on my way. I've never been one to worry about what might happen, believing instead that for every problem there's a solution – and after that there's always hope.

I've seen a lot of the world, many parts of which will never make their way onto the list of top tourist destinations. What has left a lasting impression on me has been the colourful array of local people I've met along the way. I couldn't have survived my time in India without Veer Singh who was always willing to go the extra mile. The kindness of strangers and the generosity of those with so little of their own has been humbling. My stay at Imran and Kim's guest house in Pakistan was one of those times. Admittedly, if I remove the rose-tinted glasses, I know I've also been threatened by striking workers, exploited by rip-off merchants, come too close to being blown to bits by terrorists of one stripe or another, and almost killed by the local wildlife albeit the malaria-bearing mosquito.

I know you'd like me to say I'm going to miss the life, but to be honest, my knees are already groaning at the thought of climbing another twenty flights of stairs to the top of an oil platform. If I never see another airport during the rest of my life it will be too soon, gone forever is the huge chunk of my life I have spent as 'Billy no mates', alone and lonely, kicking my heels in departures. It will also be good not to have an occupation guaranteed to send strangers into a boredom-induced coma when they ask me to explain exactly what it is I do for a living –

a question many of my immediate family are still putting off.

Looking back on my forty-five-year career, I'm sure I've accumulated a wealth of knowledge to impart to anyone proposing to follow in my professional footsteps. From it, I've mined three nuggets.

No matter how poor your language skills, learn to say 'please', 'thank you', and 'I would like a beer' in the language of the country you are visiting. Politeness costs nothing and a beer will always make a bad situation better even if it's what got you into trouble in the first place.

Whether camping or travelling to the East, no matter how limited your baggage allowance, leave room to pack some toilet rolls and your sense of humour. You'll need copious amounts of both.

And finally

If anyone tells you that their school days were the best days of their lives, they probably didn't attend a secondary modern in the 1960s.

Oh, and just in case you're wondering what the future holds for the wife and I, we've bought a farmhouse and four acres of land in South West France where we plan to go self-sufficient. I mean, what could possibly go wrong?

Printed in Great
Britain
by Amazon